TRANSCENDING 2012 WITH MEDITATION

by Dr. Joan Sprunk

Copyright 2011, self-published in Sedona, Arizona

This book is not intended to diagnose, treat, cure, or prevent any disease. While this book is intended to offer broad consumer understanding of new discoveries and technologies, it should not be construed as providing medical advice.

The Author has purchased and used all the products described in this book, but has no financial connection with any of the companies of these products.

ISBN 978-0-9886593-6-0

Transcending 2012 With Meditation

Joan Sprunk

A Dissertation in Partial Fulfillment
of the Requirements for the Degree
Doctorate of Metaphysical Liberal Arts

THE COLLEGE OF METAPHYSICAL STUDIES
Clearwater, Florida
June 2011

Contents

There Is Something Wonderful About To Happen 1
Obstacles to the Spirit World 16
The Left- vs. Right-Brained? 22
Are You Devoted? 32
Importance of the Pineal Gland 38
Time Flies (The Mayan Calendar) 47
Why Meditate? 55
Time? Who Needs Time? 62
Step 1: Getting Nowhere Fast (Learning to Sit) 64
Step 2: Putting The Pedal To The Metal 68
Step 3: Adding Fuel To The Fire 70
Step 4: Seeing The Light (Yoni Mudra) 73
Step 5: Reaping Some Benefits (Yoga Sutras) 75
Karma Yoga 79
Step 6: The Big Secret (Kriya Yoga) 83
Step 7: Fanning The Flames 86
Step 8: Got Rhythm? (Navi Kriya) 88
Yogic Sleeping & Protection 90
Step 9: Contemplating the Navel 94
Merits and Demerits of Spiritual Organizations 98
Understanding Kundalini 110
The Great Love Story 121
Revelation 125
The Excellence of Kriya Yoga 129
UFOs and Flying Saucers? 132
STEP 10: Merkaba and Heart Center Meditation 137
Party Time 140
Open Portal 141
Glossary 143
Bibliography 148
Suggested Reading 149

Acknowledgment

Though a voracious reader, the author admits a reluctance to writing. If it were not for the encouragement and editing skills of her husband, Gary, this book would not have seen the light of day.

There Is Something Wonderful About To Happen

By now everyone has heard of the "2012" revelations and the Mayan Calendar, and everyone has a different idea of what is about to happen. This book will consider what is commonly known as the "paradigm shift" and the effects which can be expected to be upon humankind and its consciousness and how humankind can help itself move positively and more rapidly toward this new consciousness. There is no intention to dwell upon Earth changes, but instead to focus upon the outcome of the new consciousness of humankind.

The Law of Attraction states that energy draws energy like itself. It is a law, just like gravity, while here on the Earth. Whatever is in our lives that we deem real has been brought here by our inner-energy vibrations calling it to us. Everyone is a mirror for what we most need to see in ourselves, and we can change our lives by altering the energy involved with our thoughts and/or emotional patterns. It is a marvelous manifestation in that we always know where we are vibrationally by simply observing our lives.

Are you in vibrational resonance with 2012, or is there dissonance in the form of resistance and fear holding you back? Do you have the commitment to be here on the Earth plane, so that when the energy shifts it doesn't shatter your body and mind? Have you integrated your dark side and anchored your light body (if you even know what that is)? The colossal energy of this shift is such that if you are not in vibrational harmony with it, it will cause chaos and even destroy your fields.

Through the seven major **chakra**s [chukru (Sanskrit) "wheel, vortex"; see Glossary in the back of this book] of every individual person, there is one **chakra** which is of particular importance; that is the Heart **chakra**. Much of what is described in this section is based upon the writings and works of **Theosophist**s [Glossary] Madame Blavatsky (1831-1891) and Alice Bailey (1880-1949).[1]

The Solar Plexus Center

Everybody except for a very few advanced souls has the Solar Plexus Center or the Solar Plexus **chakra** as their Center of Polarization, but in the immediate cosmic future the human race that continues on Earth is destined to become centered in the Heart Center. This will cause a radical change in the natural human condition, bringing a new awareness of our surroundings, and a completely different way of relating to our environment. It is what is commonly being referred to as the "shift" or the "paradigm shift".

Our present reality is focused through the Solar Plexus Center (Solar Plexus **chakra**), which functions on the third plane of mental imagery, and is concerned with the objective logical mind. This reality will change when we begin to be centered through the Heart Center (Heart **chakra**), which is centered on the fourth plane of the etheric, and is concerned with intuition.

Our consciousness is the result of the interaction of the energy of the sky and the energy of the planet Earth, and it is the solar plexus where these two major polarities meet to produce the unit of consciousness energy we call our ego. This is the Earth/Sky relationship.

These two points of energy meet at the Solar Plexus and are then passed to the Third Eye Center where it is then interpreted in a

---

[1] Excerpts from "There is Something Positive Happening in the World" ..... by Mo Hone http://www.sevenraystoday.com/somethingpositive.htm

conscious way. However, the energy can also remain below the level of awareness as unconscious impressions.

Whether we call this energy of awareness as conscious or unconscious, it is still the human consciousness condition we were born with, and continue to use throughout our lives. It only leaves us when we die, because consciousness is the energy of life itself

Because our brain is in our head, it confuses us into thinking that it is responsible for our consciousness, but it is not. The brain only organizes our perception of the energies involved and translates them into a form we can use to our advantage in general life terms.

The lower five centers, the Base, Sex, Solar Plexus, Heart and Throat, connect the brain to the external world via the senses, one for each center, and the Third Eye Center uses these sensory impressions to create awareness. Awareness is how we interpret external energies into an understandable reality.

From this we can see how the senses are intimately connected with the chakra system because they translate the energy forms around us into a way we can understand them.

Each center or chakra is solely responsible for processing a particular sense, but for us to be consciously aware of any sense that the energy of the chakra associated with it has to make a connection with the Third Eye Center.

There are connections between all of these chakras, and the energy from several of these chakras representing different senses will react with the brain to give us a more complete understanding of the external reality being experienced.

Although the energy of the Solar Plexus Center functions as sight, this energy is also responsible for what goes on in our minds: most of us think in picture images as though we are using an inner eye. It is the polarized energy working through the Solar Plexus Center which enables us to think pictorially. This reacts with the

pineal [pīnēul (Latin) "like a pine cone"] gland as the physical representation of the Third Eye Center, to give us our everyday awareness. So whether we see images through our eyes or just think in images, our brains are actually processing energy coming from the Solar Plexus Center, and the conscious energy being used to achieve this is Solar Plexus energy.

To be polarized in a particular center shows the type and quality of the conscious energy used by the Third Eye Center and brain to express awareness.

The Solar Plexus takes its name from the sun. It is the seat of our individuality at our present stage of evolution — our everyday conscious awareness as represented by our sun sign. We have learned to use the energies from the Solar Plexus Center to control our astral body or 'desire body' which is connected to the Sex Center, and which relates to our feelings rather than our thoughts. The Sex Center today works mostly through the moon sign, and these energies usually intermingle with senses connected to our sun sign or Solar Plexus individually.

The mind of the average individual today relates to other people and events through the senses corresponding to the mental plane, which function predominantly through the Solar Plexus Center. Through this center we spend our lives struggling for an identity among all the influences from our surroundings, in order to establish a firm base for our individuality, often at the expense of others who are seen as rivals. The energies of this center allow a person to rationalize their selfishness and become a responsible member of society which is also centered on the Solar Plexus level, and which is itself building a foundation of physical form where each individual is allowed certain freedom within the imposed restrictions that exist to keep this foundation grounded.

Everything that is known about the individual's awareness of this Solar Plexus Center can be transposed to the life situations in which the individual finds himself; as much as Man is a product of the society in which he exists, so is the society a collective foundation of Man's common life ideals and objectives.

For this reason social problems like crime, poverty and war can only be cured by changing the actual structure of society. Its policies must be centered on improving the situation for every individual within society, rather than sacrificing the needs of the individuals for society.

Therefore to change society, Man must change. We can now envision that Man must change by re-orientating himself to work through the Heart Center rather than the Solar Plexus Center.

If enough individuals achieve this, society will inevitably follow suit (the Hundredth Monkey effect), and a society polarized in its Heart Center will be the new ideal of everybody, caring for everyone else and working for the good of the collective soul, rather than the individual soul.

This means that humankind must change its level of consciousness, to become polarized in the heart by learning to care, to join with others through sharing. So instead of cultivating selfishness to establish an identity, that selfishness will be lost, while retaining its identity, and see others as soul mates rather than rivals.

Picture yourself as one giant octopus with billions of arms. You would not cut off or intentionally harm one of your own arms. So it is with humankind. All of humankind is likened as one giant octopus with billions of arms, and each arm is one of your soul mates. If you would not cut off one of your own arms, then why would you harm one of your own soul mates? The octopus has but one large beating Heart Center to be shared by all of the billions of arms or soul mates. So it is with the universe we live in.

The Heart Center

We are now entering a new age, the accentuation of energies released as one sign gives way to another, and is felt through all the zodiacal levels. This increase in energy will be felt by humans through their Heart Centers, and this is becoming more apparent as we move closer to the time of the "shift", as well as giving prominence to the opposing forces that attempt to stop this from happening, which are leftover energies from the Piscean Age. Humans are at the threshold of a new awareness, which will be polarized activity of the heart rather than the Solar Plexus, and the old order always struggles harder when nearing the time of its ultimate defeat.

In the future we will be working through the Heart Center, which is the world of etheric connection. Therefore we will be aware of how we are connected to our environment and will have an additional etheric sense related to touch to help us understand this new environment. We will also become more susceptible to energies originating from beyond our solar system, making us very aware of how we, as dwellers on Earth, fit into the solar system as a whole as interplanetary travel becomes a physical reality. At present we are controlled by this level but are usually unaware of it, except through the hidden workings of our conscience.

Human beings have been polarized in their Solar Plexus Centers for many millennia. Their naturally selfish personalities have been controlled by the next center up, the Heart Center, via the conscience that has been birthed through the great religions of the world. This control has been effective through linking with humanity's senses, which work on the fourth plane, the etheric. When humankind learns to become polarized in its Heart Center, it takes control of its own senses and learns to use them to benefit its life, and planetary life in general. Humankind then becomes aware of the influence of the beings who create senses: the Celestial Hierarchy of the third dimension working through the Throat Center, who we know as angels and archangels.

An individual is aware of the energies working through his Center of Polarization by comparing his conscious awareness to his unconscious motivations.

While you have been polarized in your Solar Plexus Center, your unconscious has acted through you from the level below via your Sex Center, which connects you to the traditions of your native culture, and your superconsciousness has acted from the center above, the Heart Center, through which you are connected to your conscience. As you become more used to the energies working through your Heart Center, you will learn to use the energies working through your Solar Plexus in an instinctive way, and learn to deal consciously with the energies from all three centers above the Heart, which function through the higher self. These you will recognize initially as glimpses of intuition, until you develop the ability to use the intuition as a separate sense.

The three highest centers, the Crown, Third Eye and Throat, can be considered as the source of energies which make up our higher self, just as the lower three centers, the Base, Sex and Solar Plexus form the personality, or lower self. The Heart Center holds a unique position as the mediator between these two parts of our beings at our present stage of evolution, and will continue to do so until we experience repolarization. From that point we can use the Heart Center as the main vehicle for our natural life processes, by giving it the capacity to use energies from the higher self to direct the personality in the correct use of senses.

Slowly each individual will outgrow the unconscious influences of tradition, social conventions and laws which each person has been used to, and become more aware of the conscience through which we will realize our essential role as part of the human family. Humankind will gradually lose nationalistic ideologies, religious conventions, social prejudices and the confident attitude that a lawful society is a good society. Instead, we will see all Men as equals, act compassionately towards others, and begin to feel a personal responsibility for world problems.

Many people today are already working through their Heart Centers in preparation for complete repolarization, but this in itself has no bearing on what it is like to actually be polarized through this higher center.

Such people are preparing the way for initiation into the new awareness and, although the first stage of the initiation process is often subjective and below the level of normal consciousness, this is only a prelude to repolarization: the change of polarized centers is a radical change of consciousness which cannot and will not go unnoticed. Only a very few people alive today are polarized in their Heart Center, because this level of consciousness is equivalent to **nirvana** [nurv*onu (Sanskrit) "blowing out; extinction of the self"] that is associated with the ultimate goal of all spiritually aware people.

Primitive Man, like animals, was polarized in the root chakra, which equates with the astral plane of emotions. He lived his life as part of the planet Earth's ecosystem in a semiconscious way because he was in tune with the natural planetary rhythms: he possessed low-level self-awareness.

Once humanity gained the objectivity that came with repolarization through the Solar Plexus Center, it was at about the ideal stage of its evolution. People learned to see the world in a new way with the true wisdom that is easiest to use at such crucial changeover periods. They had learned over eons how to co-operate with nature to the advantage of both, but now they could see nature as something separate. They learned how future planning could give them a better life, which lead to the development of numbers and language, mental tools that allowed them to adjust the environment.

Most importantly, the individual human began to view his surroundings in an objective fashion. He could stand back from life and see how the environment changed, learn the rhythm of these changes and by distancing himself from the outside world he could learn to control it to suit himself.

Present-day Man has become self-aware to the point that he is able to exert vast influences over his environment that has never been possible before. Man is the only creature with enough self-awareness to consciously affect and change his environment, and because of this he has isolated himself completely from other creatures and the natural world in general. In this instance the natural world is considered as the all-inclusive ecology of the planet, where each part is completely dependent on the other parts, and each part is therefore mutually an integral part of one whole system.

This is a demonstration that humans are different to all other life on Earth. Not only can the planet do without man, but also man is now learning how to exist independently from the planet Earth through his invention of biospheres, interplanetary travel and space stations. Because of this, Man is totally responsible for his personal environment, a unique position which sets us apart from every other life form on Earth.

Today human evolution is at another crucial point in its history.

Soon humankind will be learning how to cope with a new set of energies through a polarization of the Heart Center. We are about to embark on a new adventure, and enter a completely new level of consciousness, which will again be more subjective than objective. Except this time we will be on a higher level of the spiral, and without losing the individuality we have patiently developed over millennia, we will realize how important our own role will be in the evolution of not only the human species, but in the evolution of the planet and ultimately the whole solar system of which we are all an integral part. We will know this as a fact during this new changeover period because we will become intensely aware of the etheric connections which tie us to this environment.

The Etheric Body

This next stage of development for humans will lead to a more conscious application of the etheric body, with the ability to use it as naturally as we presently use our physical/astral/mental bodies. This is a difficult concept to appreciate, because eventually we will consider the outside of this etheric energy body as the outer layer of skin.

The sense of the Heart Center is touch, and so, once we are polarized through this center, our minds will be using a different type of awareness to appreciate our environment. It will be based on the idea of connections, and how our relationship with the outer world is the result of an exchange of energy, which we will think of in terms of being touched by something or somebody.

Touch is an all-over sense, which we use mostly through our hands, but covers the whole expanse of our outer layer of skin. It is also tied in with the feeling of pleasure and pain, and relates to many other sensations which we often speak colloquially as being related to 'feeling', such as feeling under the weather, how we feel about things or people, or particular situations feel familiar. It is also the feeling of separation, as experienced when a loved one or place is missed. And although touch appears to be related to the physical, and feelings appear to be related to the astral, this is confusing only because of the limitation of language. We can make a simple illustration of this.

Humans have four bodies, the physical which is concerned with action, the astral which is concerned with emotions, the mental which is concerned with thought and the etheric which is concerned with connection. The latter we can appreciate better by describing it as the connection which leads to intuitive awareness, and the higher emotions such as love which is how we often translate these flashes of intuition. We feel we know something, we feel an affinity with someone, or we feel wary about pursuing a particular course of action: these are three cases where our intuitive faculty working through our etheric body is connected to one of our lower senses, so that we are able to be intuitively aware in a way we can comprehend. In such cases, the Heart Center is utilizing the lower centers to enable our brain to process etheric energy in a way we can understand.

The Heart Center is also concerned with conscience, which is the intuition working independently of any other Center, and stops us from doing things, feeling things and thinking things, just because we feel we shouldn't. This is because the awareness of each center is controlled by the level above the one currently in use, so the astral can control the physical: "I don't want to do that". The mental can control the astral: "I shouldn't feel like that". And the etheric can control all of these by employing the conscience: " It is wrong to think/feel/do that".

The Heart Center has the ability to connect up with the energies of every other center, as the process of linking is a natural attribute. For this reason the intuition as an extension of the etheric can function and connect with every other level working through each of the other bodily centers. So as demonstrated above, it can work in conjunction with each of the lower centers: the center of action: the Base Center, the center of emotions: the Sex Center, and the center of thought: the Solar Plexus Center, plus the higher Centers. It also has the ability to work on its own, once we learn how to use this faculty.

Eventually we will discover that intuition is an independent sense through which we are able to experience the reality of our connection with other people, beings and the environment without the need to interpret it with our logical thought processes, as we have to do today.

However, when humankind starts to become conscious in the etheric, the next higher center has to be handed control. This is the Throat Center, but in practice the Throat Center works with the Third Eye and Crown Centers to form what we know as the higher self, and this triplicate action then takes charge of the whole personality, which consists of the lower four centers. When viewed separately, we can see that the higher self is actually the vehicle which is connected to our life intentions or will, our consciousness or love, and our imagination or form. The Throat chakra connects us to the realms of the Angelic Kingdom, and in particular our Holy Guardian Angel.

Today we stand at an important threshold, where we are ready to accept the new challenge in the natural evolution of our species and become polarized in the Heart Center. Slowly we will learn to rely on our intuition, which will enable us to feel which decision to make, rather than thinking it through.

We will no longer be so concerned with visual stimulation or pictorial thoughts, but have a more general awareness of our connection to our surroundings: we will feel, as in the meaning of touch but applied conceptually rather than actually, the sense of connection and separation. The easiest way we can explain this at present is through the idea of love.

With this will come a new type of conscious awareness which will be based on subjective rather than objective knowledge, intuition instead of logic. Subjective knowledge is a function of the intuition, and is derived from the connection we all have to a vast etheric web of information which can be accessed, once we learn how. This information is not knowledge as we understand it. Regular knowledge is a function of the Solar Plexus Center, which translates etheric energy into mental patterns thereby giving us a picture to understand. The main difference between information received through the intuition and through logic, is that intuition is personal knowledge, because it is how the information reacts with our own senses; giving a personal rather than general interpretation.

Objective knowledge requires reasons, subjective knowledge does not. We need not ask why; subjective knowledge just is, it exists to be used.

We don't need to prove or validate it as with objective knowledge, we don't need to know why, or how, or whether it is the same for me as for you, or whether it is the same today as it was yesterday or will be tomorrow.

Both objective and subjective knowledge can be based on personal experience, but objective experiences are usually common to everybody and are therefore easily described whereas subjective experiences are personal and often unique, making them difficult to describe. This is because objective knowledge is based on logic, which requires the participant to stand back from the situation in order that he can reason and compare the facts with others that he already knows and have decided to accept. This enables the person to say whether or not he agrees with any new facts that have been presented.

Subjective knowledge differs from this because the ideas a person believes subjectively cannot be proved, such as whether there is life after death, to give an obvious example; the person either accepts them or revokes them according to how they feel about the subject. In other words, they know what they believe to be right.

This is the crucial difference, the belief factor. If you really believe something is true, something that can never be proved or disproved, then you have faith in your belief, faith that it is true even if other people don't agree with your belief. And because you believe it, no amount of argument will alter your beliefs, because you have faith in your own judgment. Such knowledge can be called subjective knowledge.

The remarkable thing about this process is that so many people end up agreeing about things and discovering the same "facts", when really there is no chance of convincing those who don't know for themselves in the first place. This demonstrates how numerous people are working on the same path of senses, but the individual energy of their souls gives the appearance of divergence when there is none.

And in this changeover period, from an objective to subjective frame of mind, this can be difficult, and we often need to create an objective rationale where there is none, just for our peace of mind, or because our objective self needs to give itself a role, before realizing it is redundant. Therefore many channeled books may not actually be channeled so much as consisting of subjective knowledge we are all learning to tap into. Because subjective knowledge doesn't consist of irrefutable facts, but changing ideas, which others can relate to because it stimulates them into producing their own ideas.

It also becomes relevant when trying to understand the source of esoteric knowledge. Who were the Secret Chiefs behind the Golden Dawn? Who were the Masters who worked with Blavatsky to write the Secret Doctrine and establish **Theosophy**? Are the Ascended Masters still with us today, passing on snippets of wisdom? In the light of what has been said above, does it really matter? By their works, you shall know them, and if the ideas are useful and inspiring, do we need to question their validity on the strength of their apparent origins? Perhaps the prophets don't know the source of their prophecies. Because Man is so inquisitive, they have to invent a source to give themselves, as well as their adherents, some established validity.

The lesson here is that we must learn how to appreciate things for their worthiness of content, rather than their outward appearance or apparent origin. The onus of responsibility is now on each individual to decide what they believe to be right, and not to assume that an expert's opinion is the correct opinion.

We all experience "hunches", when we can feel the connection between things without understanding what that connection might be: and this is an example of the intuition working as efficiently as it can through the Solar Plexus Center. It is only when the polarized energies pass up to the Heart Center, which works through touch rather than sight, that intuition can function properly and this is how it should function; by making us physically aware of the connections between things by literally feeling them inside the mind. The brain and Third Eye Center will still translate these connections into understandable concepts, allowing this information to be channeled to those still working through their Solar Plexus.

But what if everyone worked through the Heart Center, using his or her etheric intuition? Then translation would not be necessary, each would be able to communicate through their new etheric sense, and physical life would have changed forever. This is the next evolutionary step for humanity, no less.

With this will come a new understanding of the composition of human beings as energy beings, how we are intimately connected to our outward environment; and we will finally realize our collective role as the very consciousness of the planet Earth.

This will not be learned through new scientific discoveries. It will be experienced by all, each one for themselves, and proof will no longer be required: the fact of our true spiritual existence will be part of the common human experience of life. The esoteric will become exoteric, objective knowledge will give way to subjective knowledge, and once again science will be re-united with the occult. Why? Because we will all know what we need to know, by experiencing the truth for ourselves, and this will eventually become a completely natural human ability, and lead us on to a new age and the next step in our evolution.

Obstacles to the Spirit World

Before delving into meditation techniques, I wish to caution the reader that entrance into the spirit world requires more than knowledge, desire and willpower. I would be remiss if I didn't tell about the numerous obstacles that beset you, the reader. These obstacles can be pictured as barriers to the portal to the spirit world:

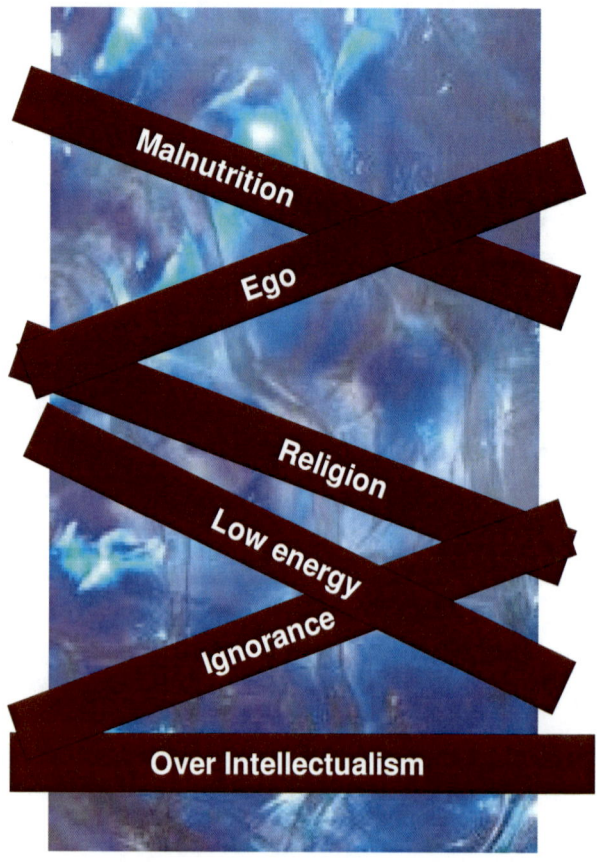

The Ego

Ego delenda est! (This is patterned after *Carthago delenda est*—Latin for *Carthage must be destroyed*). The ego is body consciousness. The ego must be overcome to experience **samadhi** [sum*odē (Sanskrit) "superconscious perception"] and liberation.

The sense of self for most people is called "ego", Latin for "I", the first person singular nominative. The ego is felt as the perceiver and doer. It thinks it's king or queen, until it suffers defeat. Of course death is the ultimate defeat, so the ego fears death and tries not to think about it.

How can the ego be dethroned? The ego can't plot its own dethronement. The only other avenue is tragedy—an accident, serious illness, disaster, or loss of loved ones. But these are beyond conscious control. So spiritual awareness comes only when the time is ripe (i.e., tragedy has struck). Have you, gentle reader, suffered tragedy?

Once the ego has been shaken to its roots, it is vulnerable. Then, the only way to destroy the ego is to love it to death, literally, by allowing the Heavenly Father/Divine Mother's love to take over the guidance of one's life, to the point where death is felt not as the end, but as a graduation to another dimension.

Religion

Religion is another stumbling block, a tender trap, to the Spirit World, as strange as that may seem. Religion is promoted as an institution that moves one closer to God, but it is instead a political tool and a business. It is diabolical! This subject is explained in the chapter *Merits and Demerits of Spiritual Organizations*.

Low energy

Low energy, low **prana** [pronu (Sanskrit) "breath"] keeps you in the lower levels of consciousness. Chronic fatigue is a precursor to illness. For most people, prolonged fatigue is puzzling. If thought of as an illness itself, Western medicine has no cure for it. People usually accept it as a part of life, and mask it by taking stimulants such as coffee, to "get them going in the morning" and sometimes to "get through the day."

If not cured, chronic fatigue leads to serious, chronic illness. Conventional Western medicine won't help you here, for it views you only as a moneymaking opportunity. You are responsible for maintaining and restoring your health. It's a learning opportunity! Consider the following.

oral pathology

Perhaps the most influential researcher and dentist of all time, Dr. Weston Price proved that the Western diet, especially sugar, causes dental cavities, and that oral pathology, especially of root-canal teeth, causes a great many, perhaps all, chronic diseases. An easy-to-read book to understand this is by Fred Hughes. *Am I Dead: ... or do I just feel like it*, Hobbies For Life, LLC, 2007.

Rife machine

Energy was used to heal in Atlantis, using crystals that were tuned to specific frequencies. That is available again through the work of Royal Raymond Rife in the 1930s. The principle is that microbes, from viruses to parasites, each has a resonant frequency. Electricity of that frequency applied to the skin will shake each kind of microbe to pieces if a strong enough current is used. "Bad" microbes are destroyed while "good" microbes are unharmed. Virtually every degenerative disease can be healed, without drugs, surgery or radiation. The possibilities are endless! Probably the best Rife machine on the market is made by AceGuru, found at http://www.rife911.com/. The author has obtained healings from asthma, pain and yeast infections using this machine.

sauna

Every person on Earth has toxins in his or her body because of pollution. A noninvasive way to remove heavy metals and organic pollutants is by being immersed in heat. Saunas are rooms designed to cause sweat. The latest sauna technology is for infrared heating. Carbon heaters are more comfortable and efficient than ceramic heaters. Avail yourself of a sauna at a health club near you, or if you can afford $2000, buy your own. I use the 2-person Malibu model, found at

http://www.rockymountainsaunas.com/index.php

Malnutrition

The Western world has the image of wealth, or having lots of "stuff." This is especially true of America, and especially true of food in America. Commercials abound with "The big gulp", "Have it your way" and "Endless shrimp." Convenience stores, fast food restaurants and a glut of supermarkets offer a cornucopia of pseudofood. Obesity is advancing rapidly, so where is malnutrition? America has a great quantity of food, but very low quality, unless you know where to look and what to look for. Organic food is more expensive but worth the higher price. Organic food used to be found only at farmers' markets or gardens, but now is in most supermarkets and health food stores. The legal definition of "organic" has been weakened, so look for "No GMOs" as well. Choose whole foods and raw foods when possible.

Do NOT use microwave ovens, which break food into free radicals. Free radicals are formed by any radiation, including nuclear fallout. The way to counteract free radicals is to ingest antioxidants. The strongest antioxidant is superoxide dismutase

(SOD), found in most green plants. The most concentrated source of SOD is chaga, also known as cinder conk (because it looks burnt), a mushroom that grows on birch and other trees. It grows slowly, in very cold habitats, and is limited largely to Siberia and northern Canada. The highest quality chaga is wild, not cultivated. It is brewed like coffee, and makes a good substitute for a cup of java in the morning. Finely ground chaga is best. I open up the 400 mg vegi caps found at http://www.taoofherbs.com/search.asp and use in a coffeemaker. Cinnamon and honey add a great taste.

The chapter "Importance of the Pineal Gland" describes the need for taking an iodine/iodide supplement. Two good sources are Iodoral 50 mg at

http://breastcancerchoices.org/order.html and Iodine Plus 2 at http://www.1-thyroid.com/order.htm

Ignorance

Scientia potentia est, a Latin maxim meaning *knowledge is power*. Everyone starts off life with *a tabula rasa*, Latin for *blank slate*, or more accurately, *erased slate*.. Much of what public education teaches is false, and only about half of English speakers are functionally literate, so knowledge is hard to come by. To find truth, the seeker must dig deep by reading, reading and more reading.

Over Intellectualism

For thousands of years, the world has been dominated by males, who tend to think more than to feel. This has led to overintellectualism in philosophy and religion. This is shown most clearly in René Descartes' famous dictum, "I think, therefore I am." Certainly there's a place for thinking in spiritual matters. But there needs to be a counterbalance, at least, in feeling. Feeling is almost entirely lacking in philosophy and religion. So, just don't read about meditation and listen to lectures about meditation.

Without diligently *experiencing* meditation, you are really just wasting your time.

The Left- vs. Right-Brained?

Our brain, like the rest of our anatomy, is made up of two halves—a left brain and a right brain. There's a big fold that goes from front to back in our brain, essentially dividing it into two distinct and almost separate parts. They are connected to each other by a thick cable of nerves at the base of each half. This sole link between the two giant processors is called the **corpus callosum** [kōrpus kul*ōsum (Latin) "firm body"].

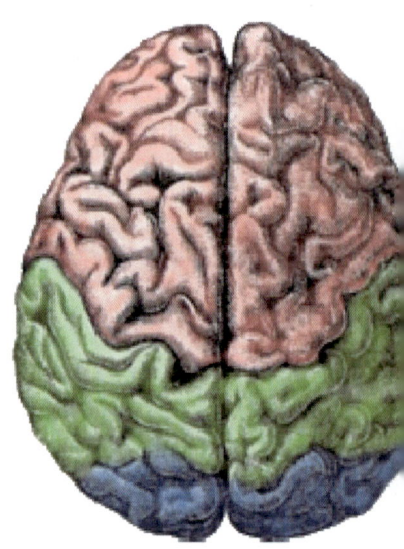

The left side of our body is "wired" to the right side of our brain, and vice versa.

Our personality can be thought of as a result of the degree to which these left and right brains interact, or, in some cases, do not interact. It is a simplification to identify "left brain" types who are very analytical and orderly. We likewise certainly know of the artistry, unpredictability and creativity of "right brain" types.

Experiments show that most children rank highly creative (right brain) before entering school. Because our educational systems place a higher value on left brain skills such as mathematics, logic and language than it does on drawing or using our imagination, only ten percent of these same children will rank highly creative by age 7. By the time we are adults, high creativity remains in only 2 percent of the population. What a pity.

We live in a culture that is still left-brain dominant. The realm of the left hemisphere (the "masculine hunter/killer" side) is logical, linear, abstract, sequential, analytical, literal and functional. To read and write, we use the skills of the left hemisphere. The right realm (the "feminine gatherer/ nurturer" side) includes intuition, creativity, metaphor, poetry, empathy, dreams, art and synthesis.

From *In Our Right Minds*™ by Dale Allen[2]:

> In our left-brain dominant culture, we define humanity according to left-brain characteristics, and we have relegated right-brain "feminine" characteristics to secondary status. We call war human nature, and peace an impractical ideal. We sing praises of women's traditional work of nurturing. Yet those who do the work of caring for children or the infirm and elderly are relegated to the lower economical, social and political rungs. Nurturing is denigrated as "non-work." We can hardly view sexuality and sensuality as holy expressions, for we have come to perceive sexuality through the lens of the left-brain with its themes of dominance, power and ownership. Our treatment of the natural world has made environmental issues like global warming an urgent concern. The United Nations has asked that the world come together for a common purpose: global investment in women and girls and the elimination of gender inequality. Our world mirrors for us the critical need for humanity to move into balance.
>
> To access our right-brain intelligence we need to shake up the fixed assumptions of our left-brain dominant perspective. It can be a challenge to get beyond the left-brain perspective we are so familiar with. We rarely question assumptions that provide

---

[2] http://daleallenproductions.com/iorm_index.htm

the foundations upon which we build our personal beliefs and in turn, our culture.

"We have been educated, formally and informally, that history begins with the written word. The first written law code is the Mesopotamian Law Code of 2350 B.C.E. Alphabetic literacy became well established across the ancient world at around 1700 B.C.E. With alphabetic literacy came a new left-hemispheric function of the human brain (we rely on the left hemisphere to read). As alphabetic literacy took hold, humanity underwent a shift into left-brain dominance and "masculine, hunter-killer" themes. New "Sky God" creation myths were written at that time that replaced the prevailing Earth-based, Goddess creation myths. Over the next thousand years, new creation myths were written in many cultures across the ancient world. Genesis was written later, in 600 B.C.E.

What we don't realize is that new foundations were laid in place at that time with those written words — foundations that are still with us today. We believe that the tenets of human existence are hierarchy, war, dominance, conquering. These tenets are left-brain oriented. Dr. Elinor Gadon outlines these foundational tenets as follows:

- A male God created the universe.
- Humans have the right to dominate nature.
- Man has the right to dominate woman.

If history begins with the written word, then indeed all history is left-brain dominant, hierarchal, patriarchal history. But human history is three million years old; the history of homo sapiens sapiens began over 100,000 years ago — it did not begin with alphabetic literacy. The Beginning is not the Word and yet, we have virtually ignored our preliterate history — the history we learn in school tells the story of territories, battles and war. When we look at what we know of Neolithic and Paleolithic history we see a time when humanity understood the creative principle to be female. We find no evidence of organized war.

"Perhaps the most provocative discovery of recent archaeological research is that nowhere in Neolithic Goddess cultures is there any sign of warfare. There is no evidence of fortifications, of violent death, invasion or conquest. We can only conclude that there was some direct relation between Goddess religion and peaceful coexistence. Neolithic Goddess culture was woman-centered, peaceful, prosperous, and nonhierarchical." Elinor Gadon

"Archaeologists ardently seek to find evidence of war in earlier societies, but there is actually no proof whatsoever of violence or war before the middle of the fifth millennium B.C.E. Although people built houses close together and lived in fairly high population density in the early urban centers, they apparently developed ways of resolving conflict and living in harmony with their environments that allowed them to share food and resources, irrigate fields, and participate in large ritual and artistic endeavors ... Goddess scholars believe that content and form cannot be separated and that the reason for the lack of violence and conflict in early societies is the presence of the active worship of the Great Mother." Vicki Noble

So there is a correlation between peaceful coexistence, a Great Mother, and right brain values in society. The Great Mother lives on, timelessly in our psyches. The archetype of the Great Mother is a part of all men and women. An archetype is an inward image in the human psyche that exerts a powerful influence on the nature of an individual personality, and in turn, on the larger culture. Poet

David Whyte says "An archetypal image is much bigger than we are – it has informed human life since the beginning of time and transcends individual experience."

> "The effect of this (Great Goddess) archetype may be followed through the whole of history, for we can demonstrate its workings in the rites, myths, symbols of early Man and also the dreams, fantasies and creative works of the ... Man of our day." Erich Neumann

> "Comparative religion ... teaches us that there is in man (beyond the psychological need for a father symbol) an equally great, or possibly even greater need: that of the divine woman who appears in many different forms throughout the world, yet remains basically the same everywhere." Raphael Patai

---

As we move into the Higher Age we find that there is a need to become more right-brained, as the "shift" will move the consciousness of humankind into the more feminine functionality of the right brain.

For men and the analytical, logical, left-brain thinking functions, it does not mean that you have to give up your masculinity to learn the right brain or feminine way of doing meditation techniques. It is just an easier way of coming into the higher state of consciousness. Would you rather go through numerous steps that may take much time to learn and in the end may not work, or would you like to achieve this in two breaths or less, and have it work every time for sure? I am sure everyone will answer that two breaths will win out over the complex process every time. To learn the more advanced methods of meditative techniques to take you to the Center of the Heart, it is necessary to learn through emotions and feelings. In the end it is bliss that you want to "feel" and to achieve.

Techniques

There are three of very simple techniques that can be used here privately, so you do not have to lose face with your male friends. In order to advance to the higher realms you must be pure in heart and have a heart filled with love. This is not just love for your children, spouse, pet, home, car, etc. You must have a heart filled with love for God and all humanity.

Pink is the color of love. OK, I know you guys do not want to talk about pink. But just give it a try privately and see where it takes your meditation.

1. Get a pink glass (a pink plastic glass is OK) or get some pink cellophane film and wrap the paper around the outside of a clear glass. The idea here is to have a pink glass, either dyed pink in the manufacturing process or made pink by the wrapping in film. Fill the pink glass with distilled water and let the glass sit in the sun for 30 minutes. Drink the water. Do this three times daily. If you don't have the time to do this three times a day then just get a pink-colored pitcher and fill it with distilled water and have it ready all the time. You can drink water from this pitcher during the day and the outcome is still the same. As long as the water has been sitting in a pink-colored container for any length of time it will work its magic.

2. Get a rose quartz crystal and carry it around with you in your pocket all day and sleep with it under your pillow during the night.

3. During your meditation think of the color pink, any shade of pink. Think of just one shade in any one meditative

period. See it all around you. See it fill the entire room. Imagine yourself breathing in the pink misty air and the pink mist filling your lungs and all the parts of your body. Do not dwell on this for more than three minutes, but at the same time do not let your mind wander.

After a period of time you will begin to notice that you have more love and compassion for the world and you will find that you are feeling more situations rather than analyzing the situations. You will be feeling the emotions of the situations and will be intuitively summing up the situations and outcomes. This is the result of using the right side of the brain.

It is also possible to heal oneself. Many who are into New Age activities think that it is necessary to go to a gifted psychic to have auras cleansed, healing techniques applied, etc. However this is not necessary. Every person is his own healer. The healing comes from within and even though the person may go to a New Age practitioner, he cannot be healed unless he believes in the healing. So if you believe in something strongly enough, the channels are opened for the healing to take place and the individual becomes the healer. Without this belief no healing would take place, no matter how gifted the practitioner is.

All colors have a meaning in the healing process. Specific colors correspond to specific moods or organs in the body. For our purposes of meditation, we will not go into all of the colors here as they correspond to each body part or mood.

Here is a meditation that I have found is easy and very efficient to use for color healing. You don't need to understand all the colors or have a lot of healing knowledge to use it. I have it indented, as it is a meditation that I found from somewhere else many years ago and do not remember where, or who wrote it, but it is wonderful and works really well.

> If you don't know what color you need, you can use this rainbow technique and it will balance your

entire body. Personally, I always use blue to remove pain of a headache and green or pure white if I need to heal something within myself. Following these instructions are more details for specific illnesses and dis-eases.

First, sit in a comfortable chair, with feet firmly planted on the floor in front of you. If you lay down you might fall asleep and not finish the technique and end up with too much color. If you stay conscious, you can control how long you do the technique. You will want to do it for only 3 to 5 minutes in the beginning. Once you are comfortable with the technique and know which color you need, you can individualize the color and work with only one at a time, such as done with individual chakras.

Breathe deeply and evenly, feeling the cleansing power of oxygen permeating your body's cells as you inhale, and the release of carbon dioxide waste as you exhale. Conscious, deep breathing cleanses the blood and cells of the body. . This also allows your spiritual Higher Self to align in the body.

Visualize the crown chakra (at the top of your head) and begin to imagine it opening as though it were the lens of a camera. Ask the Universe for all the color rays of rainbow energy to flow down through your crown chakra. Your spirit guides and guardian angels will be there to assist with this, as they are always with you. These rainbow colors are the red, orange, yellow, green, rose, blue, indigo, violet, silver, gold, and white rays. There is also infrared and ultraviolet. By stating your intent for healing they will flow from the Universe to whatever level body you need them in. Do not be concerned if you don't know how this works. Just by asking, it will happen.

As the rainbow rays flow into your crown chakra, visualize them entering your bloodstream through the arteries and permeating the cells of your entire body. This only takes a few moments to go from one end of your body to the other.

If you have a specific problem you wish to work on, you can ask for the colors to infuse that particular area of the body. The body listens to every thought you think, so just by stating what you want, it will happen. This thought/body connection is very important to know, because your every negative thought makes negative things occur, and every positive thought you have takes the body to higher levels of consciousness. The worst problem is that we confuse our own bodies by asking it to do something positive and then doubting that it can happen. In this case, please refrain from doubting the positive outcome so you don't undo the good you have just done.

In the end, balance is always the key to strive for.

Are You Devoted?

The quest for spiritual enlightenment is an ongoing process that can take many years, even many lifetimes. How far you proceed in this lifetime depends largely on what you brought with you into this incarnation.

No meditative practice is without benefit. Every moment you spent in meditation in past lifetimes has been brought forward into this lifetime. And every moment you spend in meditation in this lifetime will be added to the sum and taken forward into your next incarnation.

But wouldn't you like to obtain liberation, to conquer that process and end the relentless birth and death process of repeated incarnations? It is possible. It takes a lot of dedication and devotion **bhakti** [buktē (Sanskrit) "devotion"]. You cannot reach the goal of enlightenment and the conscious exit of your life from this body **mahasamadhi** [muh*o-sum*odē (Sanskrit) "great **samadhi**"] without dedicating your life to the quest for God, devotion.

You will have all the tools you need in these lessons to obtain your goal. It is then a matter of devotion to your daily routine in your life to obtain the most important goal a person ever has in their incarnations. Where there is a will there is a way. If you want something badly enough you will find a way to get it.

You will first learn the ancient, traditional techniques of meditation, which have been used for ages in the East. Then we will move into a new type of meditation for the new age which is upon us. This new meditation will combine various aspects of the ancient techniques into new techniques which will result in the polarization of the Heart Center to better prepare us for the new age which is coming upon us quickly.

It is not possible to have the complete benefit of the Heart Center meditation without the proper foundation in the ancient techniques of meditation.

I once read an article that was published in the *Hindustan Times, Sacred Corner* on February 19, 2004. The title of the article was "Bhakti — The Science of Devotion". It is an eye-opening article and I quote it below:

> Devotion is the most common **yoga** technique in the world, though it is rarely called "**yoga**." The focus of desire on a spiritual ideal is so common that the great religions are called "belief systems" or "faiths," as if nothing else but devotion exists in spiritual practice. Why is devotion so important?
>
> Placing an ideal to strive for in our heart is more than a simple psychological mechanism. Directed emotional energy has great power. The act of desiring a high ideal is a transforming power. This alone will be changing us inside before we ever sit to meditate. Devotion is the first **yoga** practice, and the fire that lights all advanced **yoga** practices.
>
> Like any of our spiritual abilities, devotion is a natural product of our opening nervous system. It is the most visible spiritual ability in everyone. There is a branch of **yoga** called **bhakti**, that is concerned with optimizing desire and devotion to the highest level of spiritual effectiveness. Having a basic knowledge of the methods of devotion can have a huge effect on the course of our spiritual life.
>
> **Bhakti** means, "love of God, " which means love of our highest ideal or truth. Whatever that is for us, loving it will change us, and inspire us to pursue spiritual methods. We know that love changes us. When we care about something or someone more than ourselves, we are changed. As the Beatles

sang, "All you need is love." If we had listened, the Earth would be paradise by now. We are not there yet, but we are on the way. Love was the right thing then, and it is the right thing now.

Who decides what our highest ideal is? Our **guru** [gurū (Sanskrit) "dispeller of darkness"]? Our mullah? Our priest? Our rabbi? There will be plenty of suggestions. Everyone wants us to love their ideal. It is a game we have played for thousands of years. Love my ideal, will you please? Or else!

Only you can choose your ideal. It is what burns brightest in your heart. Maybe it is Jesus. Maybe Krishna. Maybe Allah. Maybe your **guru**. Maybe the inner light. It can be anything. Only you can know. It is personal. You will know it when you see it — all goodness, all progress, projecting no harm. It will lead you home to peace and bliss.

In the language of devotion, the chosen ideal is called, **ishta** [ishtu (Sanskrit) "an ideal"]. If nothing burns bright inside, it is okay. You are reading these words, so you are moving toward your ideal. Your highest ideal is in your studying and in your interest to practice **yoga**. Your ideal is in you, and your desire is leading you to it.

Devotion begins with that very first question: "Is there something more?"

First it is a fuzzy notion, a vague desire, a sense of wonder. That opening brings knowledge in. Who knows from where it will come? We grab on and start doing some practices. Some inner experiences come, some blissful silence, some clarity. We read the scriptures, and words that were just words before come alive with radiant meaning. Gradually, our ideal becomes clearer. We find ourselves in a relationship with what is happening inside us.

Devotion is getting stronger, and we are falling deeper into the divine game.

There is a method to devotion. There are always desires. We want this thing. We want money. We want a lover. Even anger and frustration are desires — desires that have hit a wall, so the energy goes haywire, sending us hither and yon. The method of devotion is in redirecting our desires. This is possible when there is silence inside from daily meditation. Our sense of self goes underneath the desires bubbling up, so we can see them like objects. Then we can nudge them toward our ideal. We favor our ideal when emotional energy comes surging up.

Suppose we are stuck at a traffic light, frustrated because we are late. A lot of emotional energy is there. We can take our frustration and redirect it. We let the red light go as the object of our frustration, and bring in our ideal as the object. It is like meditation. We easily favor one thought object over another. So now we are frustrated about our ideal. "Ideal! Why am I not merged with you yet? I am frustrated!" Now we have real motivation not to miss daily meditation. Not only that, our emotional energy, directed in this way, produces spiritual changes inside. It opens our nervous system. It is ironic that we can't change a red light with our emotions, but we can open our nervous system to God.

This method can be done with every emotion. We can quietly cultivate a habit of devotion in life so the wheels of devotion will always be turning. More spiritual intensity will come up. It is called "**tapas** [tupus] (Sanskrit) "intensity"." Intensity is devotion that never stops, like an endless flame in us, and all of life becomes spiritual practice.

Mother Theresa of Calcutta said she saw Jesus in the eyes of every child she helped. That is intensity.

Remember the method of devotion in your daily life, especially if you find yourself in a storm of emotional energy. That is prime time for devotion. Just an awareness of the method of devotion will open doors inside when emotions flare up.

The great nineteenth-century saint, Ramakrishna Paramhansa, was a master at creating huge waves of devotion. He would sob on the floor at the statue of his Divine Mother, craving her inner touch. The more desperate he got the more he would direct it toward his ideal. He seemed like a crazy man. All the while his devotion was working like a laser beam, burning every obstruction in his nervous system. By devotion alone he became the divine.

Devotion is a systematic approach to the application of a specialized kind of knowledge. **Bhakti** is the science of devotion — a powerful science indeed.

So we take this information to heart and turn all of our ordeals in our daily life into a God quest filling our lives with **bhakti** — *devotion*. You may say that this is not practical for you in your life. Remember that where there is a will, there is a way. Here are a few suggestions that can be put into everyday use. They may seem a little strange at first and you may even forget to do them in the heat of your emotions taking control, but the more you are conscious of them and make a conscious effort to put them into practice, the closer you will be drawn to the divine.

- Instead of listening to popular music, listen to Sanskrit chants. Load them into your iPod. Keep them playing softly for long periods of time.
- Do not argue with others. Instead of engaging in the argument, stare at your adversary's Third Eye and chant

inwardly several times **OM** [ŌM (Sanskrit) "**mantra** for primordial vibration of God"], or chant *I LOVE YOU* inwardly while focusing on their Third Eye.

- Read books that will educate you on spiritual matters. A great book to start with is *Autobiography of a Yogi,* by Paramhansa Yogananda. Read it again if it has been awhile since you read it. Another great book is Patanjali's *Yoga Sutras"*

- Turn off the television. Get in the habit of watching less and less of television.

- Have a sphere of friends that are advantageous to your spiritual development. Drop the drinking buddies.

- Diet is important to inner spirituality development. Stop eating meat from slaughtered animals. Animals have a consciousness also and that consciousness is now affecting your consciousness. You have evolved above the animal incarnations, so do not take the animal back inside you. Remember you are what you eat.

- Remember that your body is a temple of God. God is within. Treat it like a temple and do not defile it with drugs, cigarettes, alcohol, and slaughtered animals.

Importance of the Pineal Gland

Devotion is a major factor. However, there is another major factor which many people may not be aware of. That is the calcification of the **pineal** gland. It is important that we rectify the problems encountered in this day and age of toxins and poisons in order to proceed with "self-realization". No matter how many hours one may put into meditation, it will not be effective for enlightenment or self-realization unless the **pineal** gland is able to receive the vibrations that come its way through the techniques being learned to stimulate it. **Pineal** derives its name from its shape, which is like a tiny pine cone. All of the meditation techniques taught here will direct the energy to the Third Eye and/or crown chakra. The **pineal** gland was known in ancient times as the sacred eye. Therefore it is important that the **pineal** gland be healthy for effective meditation and to achieve **samadhi**.

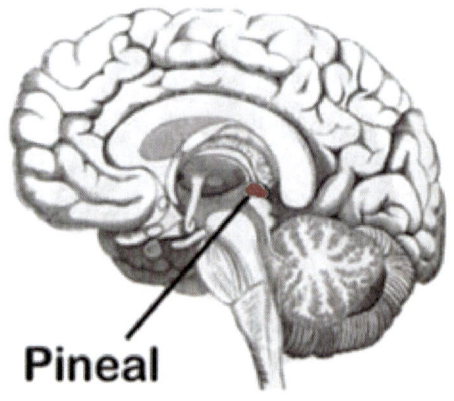

*Up until the 1990s, no research had ever been conducted to determine the impact of fluoride on the **pineal** gland – a small gland located between the two hemispheres of the brain that regulates the production of the hormone melatonin. Melatonin is a hormone that helps regulate the onset of puberty and helps protect the body from cell damage caused by free radicals.*

It is now known – thanks to the meticulous research of Dr. Jennifer Luke from the University of Surrey in England – that the

pineal *gland is the primary target of fluoride accumulation within the body.*

*The soft tissue of the adult **pineal** gland contains more fluoride than any other soft tissue in the body – a level of fluoride (~300 ppm) capable of inhibiting enzymes.*

*The **pineal** gland also contains hard tissue (hydroxyapatite crystals), and this hard tissue accumulates more fluoride (up to 21,000 ppm) than any other hard tissue in the body (e.g. teeth and bone).*[3]

Other than regulating vital hormones, the **pineal** gland is known to serve an esoteric function. It is known by mystic groups as the "Third Eye" and has been considered by many cultures to be part of the brain responsible for spiritual enlightenment and the "link to the divine". Is enlightenment out of bounds for the modern man?

*"In the human brain there is a tiny gland called the **pineal** body, which is the sacred eye of the ancients, and corresponds to the Third Eye of the Cyclops. Little is known concerning the function of the **pineal** body, which Descartes suggested (more wisely than he knew) might be the abode of the spirit of man."*[4]

Excerpts from "Iodine and Chelation"[5]:

Humanity is traveling down a deadly path. Awaiting each and every child born on the planet is a life doomed to being poisoned. There is "overwhelming evidence that every child, no matter where in the world he or she is born, will be exposed, not only from birth, but from conception, to man-made chemicals that can undermine the child's ability to reach its fullest potential—chemicals that interfere with the natural chemicals that tell tissues how to develop

---

[3] http://vigilantcitizen.com/?p=4051
[4] Hall, Manly P. 1928. *The Secret Teachings of All Ages.* Self-published.
[5] International Medical Veritas Association,
http://www.alkalizeforhealth.net/Liodine2.htm

and construct healthy, whole individuals according to the genes they inherited from their mothers and fathers," says Dr. Theo Colborn, Senior Program Scientist, at the World Wildlife Fund. This chapter offers a hugely important answer, a guardian angel in chemical form that we can and actually have to use in the highly toxic age we are all living through. Every pregnant woman should be using iodine and magnesium chloride applied transdermally [through the skin] to initiate protective action from even before conception.

Heavy metals poison us by disrupting our cellular enzymes, which run on nutritional minerals such as magnesium, zinc, and selenium. Toxic metals kick out the nutrients and bind their receptor sites, causing diffuse symptoms by affecting nerves, hormones, digestion, and immune function. The heavy metals most often implicated in human poisoning are lead, mercury, arsenic, and cadmium but uranium is playing catch up since depleted uranium became the favorite armament of the United States military. Once in the body, they compete with and displace essential minerals such as iodine, zinc, copper, magnesium, and calcium, and interfere with organ system function.

No where is this process more evident than in the case of the halides, which are all antagonistic elements to iodine, meaning they will impede the absorption of iodine. Heavy metals get stored in the same receptors that are looking for iodine. Almost all of us are exposed to bromine and fluorine and are storing these toxic halides in our iodine-deficient receptors. The mechanism of iodine in the cells is very ancient and lacking of specificity, in fact, cells are not able to distinguish iodide from other anions of similar atomic or molecular size, which may act as "pseudo-iodides": bromide, fluoride, chlorine, thiocyanate, cyanate, nitrate, pertechnate, perchlorate.

In the 1960s iodine added to bread increased the average daily intake 4-5 times RDA levels.

Then they took the iodine out of the bread and some medical idiot substituted bromide, a bio-poison in its place. There are actually four halogens: iodine, bromine, fluorine and chlorine. All these halogens use the same receptors in the body. Therefore if a person's diet is deficient in iodine the iodine receptors in the thyroid and stomach, for example, may fill up with bromine which is common in grains, bleached flour, sodas, nuts and oils as well as several plant foods. Iodine is depleted by bromine, which is used as a spray on fruits and vegetables, in baked goods, as a fumigant, and in Prozac, Paxil and many other pharmaceutical drugs. Chlorine, fluorine, and fluoride are chemically related to iodine, and compete with it, blocking iodine receptors in the thyroid gland.

Iodine intake immediately increases the excretion of bromide, fluoride, and some heavy metals including mercury and lead. Bromide and fluoride are not removed by any other chelator or detoxifying technique.[emphasis added]

Dr. Kenezy Gyula Korhaz states that iodine chelates heavy metals such as mercury, lead, cadmium and aluminum and halogens such as fluoride and bromide, thus decreasing their iodine-inhibiting effect especially of the halogens. Iodine has the highest atomic weight of all the common halogens (126.9). **Iodine is the only option when it comes to removing these toxic haloids from the thyroid and even the pineal gland where fluoride concentrates** [emphasis added], especially when there is a deficiency in iodine in the body. In an age of increasing radioactivity and toxic poisoning specifically with fluoride, chlorine and bromide, and even mercury, iodine is a necessary mineral to protect us from harm for immediately these toxic substances will increasingly flow out of the body in the urine.

Many of us are forced or conditioned to drink fluoridated water and also brush our teeth with fluoride. Could an iodine deficiency be related in some way to the current epidemic of hypothyroidism, breast, and prostate cancers? Are government health officials poisoning the public with fluoride and bromide, aspartame and mercury, and even with rocket fuel, just to name a few things? Yes this is exactly what they are doing, and they are feeling quite defensive about it.

> *There is growing evidence that Americans would have better health and a lower incidence of cancer and fibrocystic disease of the breast if they consumed more iodine. A decrease in iodine intake coupled with an increased consumption of competing halogens, fluoride and bromide, has created an epidemic of iodine deficiency in America.*
>
> *Dr. Donald Miller Jr.*

Dr. David Brownstein says that fluoride inhibits the ability of the thyroid gland to concentrate iodine, and research has shown that fluoride is much more toxic to the body when there is iodine deficiency present. When iodine is supplemented the excretion rate of the toxic halides bromide, fluoride and perchlorate is greatly enhanced. Brownstein says that after only one dose of iodine the excretion of fluoride increased by 78% and this is very important for those who are drinking fluoridated water or are taking medicines with fluoride in them; bromide excretion rates increased by 50%. Our environment is loaded with the toxic halides bromine and fluorine and up to now we have had no way to detoxify the body of these thyroid poisons.

> *No chelation or detoxification protocol can afford to ignore iodine.*

Over the last 2 decades bromine has contaminated our bread. Bromine blocks thyroid function and may interfere with the anticancer effect of iodine on the breast. Now, the risk for breast cancer is 1 in 8 and increasing 1% per year. Chlorine also blocks iodine in the body, so chlorinated water (both drinking and bathing) should best be avoided when possible. (See chapter on sodium thiosulfate for chlorine neutralization) Iodine increases mobilization of bromine from storage sites with increased urinary excretion of bromide. Elevated bromide levels were observed in urine and serum samples, twenty times the levels reported in the literature in normal subjects.

Patients who experience side effects while on orthoiodo-supplementation are often excreting large amounts of bromide in the urine.

Chloride competes with bromide at the renal level and increases the renal clearance of bromide, thus magnesium chloride is ideal for magnesium supplementation. Some patients require up to 2 years of iodine therapy to bring post-loading urine bromide levels below 10 mg/24 hr, if chloride load is not included in the bromine detoxification program. Rapid mobilization of bromine from storage sites with orthoiodo-supplementation combined with increased renal clearance of bromide with a chloride load often causes side effects. Increasing fluid intake and adding a complete nutritional program minimizes these side effects.

Dr. Abraham noted that in some patients the excretion of lead, cadmium and mercury increased several fold after only one day of iodine supplementation and that increased aluminum excretion was noted about a month after beginning supplementation. Orthoiodo-supplementation induces a detoxification reaction in some patients with high bromide levels. The symptoms include increased body odor and cloudy urine. The body odor lasts one to two weeks, but the cloudy urine may last several months before clearing up. Side effects can be minimized by increasing fluid intake. Increased fluid facilitates the excretion of excess iodine and the bromides, fluorides and heavy metals that the iodine displaces. Dr. Abraham also reported that the administration of magnesium in daily amounts up to 1200 mg eliminated the body odor but not the cloudy urine.

Released bromide from storage sites can induce decreased thyroid function, bromide being a potent goitrogen.

In the United States especially people will want to note that iodine also is protective and effective at eliminating perchlorate from the body. Perchlorate, the explosive ingredient in solid rocket fuel, has leaked from military bases and defense and aerospace contractors' plants in at least 22 states, is contaminating drinking water, dairy milk, produce and many other foods and plants affecting millions of Americans. In the past year, CDC scientists have found that a significant number of women are at risk of thyroid hormone depression from perchlorate exposure. Perchlorate impairs the thyroid's ability to take up iodide and produce hormones critical to proper fetal and infant brain development. Further, studies show that breast milk may have even more worrisome levels of perchlorate.

The EPA's proposed safe exposure level for the rocket fuel contaminant perchlorate is not protective of public health. In the past year, CDC scientists have found that a significant number of women are at risk of thyroid hormone depression from perchlorate exposure.

Now how does all of this effect us for 2012? Many are concerned with 2012 and claiming that the Mayan calendar ends in 2012 and that therefore it is the end of the world. 2012 is not the end of the *world*. It is the end of an *age*. That means that the world and humankind within the world is being transformed.

Carlos Barrios is an anthropologist, historian and investigator who has been initiated as a Mayan ceremonial priest and spiritual guide. Carlos Barrios says that the transformation will be both spiritual and physical and that this transformation started in 1987. He says that we are in a spiritual transition from the rule of materialism, greed, and enmity to a new period of cooperation and peace – but not without difficulty. The current oligarchy is happy with what they have and don't want to give it up, and they are powerful. The Mayans claim that 2012 marks the end of the period of the fourth sun and the beginning of the fifth sun.

Carlos points out that adversarial revolution against the ruling class will not work. **It is up to those who want this shift to connect with others of like mind and begin actively creating networks of real cooperation** [emphasis added]. The old will crumble. The new period will dawn with its growing pains, the severity of which depends on our ability to accept what is happening and go with the flow. This, he says, requires evolving to unconditional love, with an open and simple heart, forgiveness, and cooperation with less ego competition.

So the next obvious question is, what does all of this have to do with the **pineal** gland? The **pineal** gland is considered to be the doorway to the higher self. Psychics consider it to be the link for interdimensional experiences. It is associated with what is known as the Third Eye or sixth **chakra**, which is the doorway to higher consciousness and bliss.

An unusual psychiatrist, professor of medicine at University of New Mexico, and a practicing Buddhist, Dr. Rick Strassman, MD, has written a book based on actual human studies of people under the psychedelic drug DMT, titled *DMT, The Spirit Molecule*. He has discovered, among other things, that the **pineal** gland is a source of DMT production during birth and at death, and during near-death or mystical experiences. This chemical approach corroborates the idea of the **pineal** gland as a portal, where the spirit passes through to other dimensions, either entering this physical realm or leaving it.

South American and Central American shamans use ayahuasca, an herbal potion that stimulates DMT for psychological healing and spiritual initiation ceremonies. They have expanded their ceremonies with ayahuasca by traveling throughout the world or opening their local facilities to nonnatives. They are doing this urgently in anticipation of 2012. Their desire is to jump start and expand individuals' consciousness so the transition of consciousness will be facilitated and incorporate as many as possible.

The human **pineal** gland grows in size until about 1–2 years of age, remaining stable thereafter, although its weight increases gradually from puberty onwards. The abundant melatonin levels in children are believed to inhibit sexual development. When puberty arrives, melatonin production is reduced. According to Vincent Iannelli, MD, puberty is occurring at an increasingly earlier age in children.

Hormones have a huge effect on the paranormal. There is much about the human body that actually does affect the paranormal, and psi abilities. The hormones basically run almost everything in the body, if you include endorphins, and many others. The hormones tend to peak at puberty, which is why we see so many psychic children. Most children's psychism peaks at puberty, and then abilities taper off over the years. Some do have abilities at a young age, but this is due to a completely different reason. Since puberty is occurring at an earlier age in children these psi abilities are likewise showing up at a younger age.

The psi activities that occur with puberty-aged children are usually related to poltergeist activity and ghostly hauntings, although other activities can occur. These children may or may not show other psychic abilities.

At the same time that the onset of puberty is arriving, the melatonin production is reduced. Melatonin is an anti-oxidant and many studies are still underway as to the use of it as a supplement.

The point here is that it is time to encourage health, meditation and spiritual growth to get in shape for the approaching 2012 transformation. This means having a fluoride-free and healthy **pineal** gland.

Time Flies (The Mayan Calendar)

Summary of the *Mayan Calendar Conversion Codex,* by Ian Lungold:[6]

Carl J. Calleman Ph.D., is a biochemical scientist from Sweden. He has worked in labs performing microbiology experiments. Most of his work was investigating how pollution causes disease to proliferate. However he has trained his attention on the Mayan calendar to see what correlations or sets of facts could be proven, not just "studied" as the archeologists have done. What he uncovered with his newfound "hobby" is quickly changing the world and the way we live with it. Dr. Calleman has scientifically proven the Schedule of Creation and Evolution over the last 16.4 billion years (from the Big Bang forward).

Dr. Carl J. Calleman, began studying the Mayan calendar with empirical scientific techniques which he had learned and practiced in his 30-year career as a microbiologist. Essentially what he discovered was a schedule of the evolution of consciousness over the last 16.4 billion years. The information he discovered shows a repeating pattern of consciousness that produces physical effects in the evolution of physicality, life forms and events in history.

The Mayan calendar can now be shown to be not an instrument for tracking the procession of time as we consider it, but as a meter and the measure of the evolution of consciousness.

Calleman's research of the Mayan civilization and the writings that were carved in stone throughout Meso-America disclose that the Mayan calendar is built of nine different levels. Each of these nine levels is the running of a process of the development of a type

---

[6] www.mayanmajix.com

of consciousness through 13 equally divided stages or intentions on the part of consciousness. The Maya described the 13 sections as seven periods of day or experiences of new fresh consciousness, and six periods of dark or application of what has now become part of consciousness.

Here is a quick run-through of the previous cycles and the consciousness that each level produced:

1. **Cellular cycle** — beginning 16.4 billion years ago, developed the consciousness of **Action/Reaction**.

2. **Mammalian cycle** — beginning 820 million years ago, developed the consciousness of **Stimulus/Response**.

3. **Familial cycle** — beginning 41 million years ago, developed the consciousness of **Stimulus/Individual Response**.

4. **Tribal cycle** — beginning 2 million years ago, developed the consciousness of **Similarities/Differences**.

5. **Cultural cycle** — beginning 102,000 years ago, developed the consciousness of **Reasons**.

6. **National cycle** — beginning in the year 3115 B.C., developed the consciousness of **Law**.

7. **Planetary cycle** — beginning in the year 1755 A.D., developed the consciousness of **Power**.

8. **Galactic cycle** — beginning January 5, 1999, developing the consciousness of **Ethics**.

9. **Universal cycle** — beginning February 10, 2011, will be developing the unlimited ability of Conscious **Co-Creation**.

Looking at the timing and the product of each of the nine cycles listed above, we can see an orderly progression of the development of consciousness and our abilities to interact with the universe.

During the First cycle, all of the physical laws, chemical compounds, star fields, then solar systems and planets were developed.

In the Second cycle, individual cells which were the product of the Cellular cycle started developing stimulus/response and the survival mechanism. Stimulus/response differs from action/reaction in the amount of consciousness present.

The Third cycle was the recognition of individual consciousness and the establishment of the family relationship (recognition of individuals) rather than a herd, school or flock mentality.

In the Fourth cycle, consciousness developed the tool, which we call "The Mind" to detect the similarities and differences in our experience.

During the Fifth cycle, the leading edge of consciousness was developing reasons for any and every thing. These "Shared Reasons," are the basis of all culture.

In the Sixth cycle, the concept of law or right and wrong developed.

In the Seventh cycle, which is from 1755 A.D. to present, we have been gathering power derived from natural laws.

Each time that this pattern has repeated it has done so 20 times faster than the previous cycle.

This quite handily explains why time seems to be speeding up. Time is not speeding up. It is creation itself that is speeding up with more and more happening in less and less time.

We now know exactly where we are in this repeating pattern. This information makes it possible to put forth educated guesses as to the content of our future. This is similar to using a map when you are traveling. In this case, we now have a roadmap of time, consciousness and events.

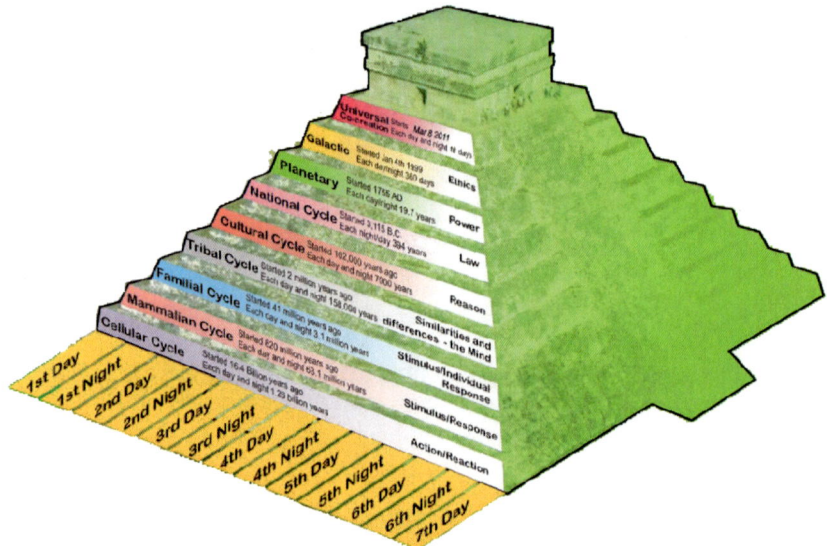

So what does this mean to us?

This can best be understood by using the metaphor of planting a seed.

During the First Day there is the seed itself — an inception, a new beginning or impetus to change or flow in a new direction where new perceptions become available. That if followed by the First Night which is an opportunity to apply the enlightenment just received from Creation's flow. This would be the germination of the seed planted in the dark soil or the developments of new points of view.

The Second Day is when duality is put on display. The seed sprouts up out of the ground and displays two leaves. The essential duality is always a new viewpoint that is overriding the "old" consciousness. As it has come down in human history, this has always been a time of civil turmoil. We have just completed the Second Night of the Galactic cycle from December 19, 2001, to December 14, 2002. The Second Night is a period of dark when polarized factions come to blows over their differences.

The Third Day is another period of Light. The seed's root system develops and the second set of leaves will be a permanent part of the plant. It is the establishment of the new consciousness as viable. In human history, lies or failed systems are disclosed so that progress is not blocked. Hold onto your hat as the truths pour forth from mid 2002 through most of 2003. The Third Night is another period of Dark. The seedling set of leaves are dropped from the plant as another set of leaves spring from the top. These are at 90 degrees from the last set. In human history failed systems have been jettisoned, usually by force, during this section.

The Fourth Day, another period of Light and in a plant's life, the tap root grows deep to firmly attach the plant while the stock thickens and branches form. It is a period of expansion of the foundations laid. In human history the "new" point of view and way of doing things takes dominance. For instance the empire of Greece was built during this section. The Fourth Night is a period of Dark once again or the application of new procedures. During this time a plant is multiplying its leaves and root system like mad. In human history it has usually been a period of rebuilding and a time of healing.

The Fifth Day is a period of Light and, in fact, is the brightest period of light in the entire cycle. In a plant's life this is when new chemicals are produced that carry the message to form buds. In human history, it was this section when Art was invented, the message of Jesus moved over the Earth, Mr. Einstein discovered the theory of relativity and when America rose to world power with the victory of WWI. The Fifth Night or period of dark that follows is also the darkest period of each cycle.. In a plant's life this is the growth of the bud. In your history, this was puberty. In all of human history this has been a time of great physical hardship or major conflicts, i.e., the Ilionian Ice Age, the Neanderthals going extinct, Rome falling, and WWII are glaring examples.

The Sixth Day we return to a period of "Enlightenment." This is the time of flowers for the plant. For you personally, it was adolescence. In human history this was the creation of the first tools, the first attempts at agriculture and constructed shelter, the Renaissance and, most recently, the Flower Children Movement of the 60's. The Sixth Night, one last period of Dark in the cycle follows. In the plant's life the flowers wilt and die setting the stage for fruit development or of seedpods that will dry. This is what happened to the Maya civilization right on cue. Throughout human history there have been conflicts and revolts during this period, the most recent of these having been the Viet Nam War.

The Seventh Day is once again a period of Light, a time of readiness for something new and different, a time of ascension or going from one level to the next higher level. The plant spreads the seeds or drops the fruit to begin again a thousand times over. In human history it was during these repeating sections that Consciousness developed Homo Sapiens, agriculture and domesticated herds, signed treaties to establish the sovereignty of nations and their people, and put up the Internet thereby creating a planetary consciousness in 1992.

This pattern of Creation, an action plan, can be seen happening everywhere in the universe — from subatomic particles to galaxies. Over and over: "As above, so below." Notice that we go from a Light section to another new Light section. In other words, after the seventh day, there is no seventh night? We begin the next cycle with another day. So, you see the deck is stacked. Creation is on our side and always has been.

It is also important to note that this chart in no way conflicts with either the Creationist or Evolutionist points of view. In fact, it marries the two. No matter how uncomfortable that concept may be at the outset, the facts that Creation has evolved are indisputable because that evolution and schedule continues today. In fact, the evolution of all consciousness has accelerated to such a degree that we can watch it unfold step by step as in time-lapse photography.

To "shed even more light" (pardon the pun), on the events that occur during the days and nights of a particular cycle, let's use the Sixth Cycle or National Cycle as an example and use religious development as our "event" taking place during each one of the 13 sections or Seven Days and Six Nights. Only, in this instance, we are going to focus primarily on the Days of this cycle since the Days are the periods of enlightenment when new perceptions are gained by Consciousness.

The First Day of the National Cycle occurred from 3115 BC to 2721 BC. This was the time that the Sumerians worshipped An or Anu. Anu was seen as an omnipotent Creator God who had to share his space with a host of household, workplace, weather and nature gods of all kinds.

The Second Day of the National Cycle occurred from 2326 BC to 2938 BC. During this section Abraham moved to Cana in 2300 BC.

The Third Day of the National Cycle was from 1538 BC to 1144 BC. This was the time of Moses and the beginning of Monotheism (The Truth coming into sharper focus).

The Fourth Day of the National Cycle was from 749 BC to 355

BC. Isaiah was from the year 748 BC; Buddha from 552 BC; Confucius from 551 BC; Zoroaster from 550 BC; Pythagoras from 550 BC, Deuteron- Isaiah from 550 BC.

The Fifth Day of the National cycle was from 40 AD to 434 AD. During this period Paul took the message of Jesus to the world and Christianity was born. Buddhism started in China in 60 AD and the Talmudic and Judaism religions began at this time. In 40 AD Quetzalcoatl, the Maya Creator god, appeared in Teotihuacán as a Christ-like personage with a very similar message. (The Fifth Night of the National Cycle occurred from 434 AD to 829 AD and was when Islam was inspired in 632 AD.)

The Sixth Day of the National Cycle was from 829 AD to 1223 AD. At this time there was a general expansion of Christianity to Northern and Eastern Europe. The Crusades and the development of the Papacy happened here as well as the second Quetzalcoatl where in the Maya/Toltec city of Chichen Itza walked the Earth. (The Sixth Night was when the second wave of Islam came in from 1223 AD to 1617 AD.)

The Seventh Day of the National Cycle occurred from 1617 AD to 2011 AD. During this period, Christianity expanded once again starting with the Pilgrims in 1620 AD.) We could go through other events such as scientific principles, communication methods, the development of political ideals, and we would see that the developments in each field conform to this same schedule. In fact, everything we know of what happened follows this schedule. There is no mistake. This is no 16.4 billion-year-long coincidence!

Why Meditate?

So you are a good person who works hard, but still lack money, a mate, health or happiness? You may pray for these things, but your prayers aren't answered. What to do? You feel you need to be more in tune with God. Possibly the most important instruction in the Bible is when Jesus said, "Seek ye first the kingdom of heaven, and then all the rest will be added unto you as well." (Matthew 6:33) That is, if you find God, then everything you need will be yours. What a promise! A parallel passage from the **Bhagavad Gita** [Buguvud Gētu (Sanskrit) "Song of the Blessed One"], the "bible" of India, is when Krishna said, "To men who meditate on me as their very own, ever united to me by incessant worship, I supply their deficiencies and make permanent their gains." (9:22) So there is the answer—meditate.

But what is meditation? Wikipedia gives a definition: "Meditation is a holistic discipline during which time the practitioner trains his or her mind in order to realize some benefit.

Meditation has been around since ancient times. Proof is found in Indian artifacts of **Tantra** [tuntru (Sanskrit) "two woven together"], which speaks of esoteric disciplines, written 5000 years ago. Researchers suggest that primitive hunting and gathering societies may have been the ones to have discovered meditation's many different states of consciousness while gazing into the flames of their fires. Meditation has evolved over thousands of years into a structured practice that people use to this day.

The **Rig Veda** [Rig Vādu (Sanskrit) "praise knowledge"], the earliest recorded religious literature of Northern India, written about 1000 B.C.E., in an Indo-European language, describes in detail the ecstasy experienced in meditation.

In the **Tao**ist work, **Tao** Te Ching of China, written four or five centuries B.C.E., formalized meditation is also recorded. The **Tao**ists emphasized breath control in meditative practice and believed it to be a skill to be achieved in many stages. The ultimate stage or goal is to be able to breathe without inhaling or exhaling—to the point of the complete cessation of the pulse. If one were able to arrive at this stage successfully, it was said they would transcend conscious thought to the state of what they called the Great Quiescence, or the highest form of enlightenment and the goal of **Tao**ist meditation.

The **Upanishads** [Ūp*anishadz (Sanskrit) "sitting down near" (secret doctrine)] of India give a detailed description of the psychology of meditation as being the way to control the physical senses and actions, thereby freeing oneself from the bondage of the external world. The **Upanishads** speak of the cultivation of a one-pointed mind through meditation as being the prelude to attaining God consciousness.

Kabbalistic literature and teachings, as well as biblical references to prayer and meditation throughout both the Old and New Testaments, cite setting self apart from the masses and going to a still, quiet place—within and without—as a source of mystical communication with God.

Thousands of years ago, Patanjali, an Indian sage of legend, described the process by which the capacity to meditate is actualized. He called it "Self Realization" since, in the state of meditation, he experienced an absolute awareness of his "Self".

The mechanism by which "Self Realization" occurred was a closely kept secret that was handed down from a **guru** to his disciple after long penances, discipline and purification.

In the 14th century the great saint Gyaneshwara of Central India took permission from his **guru** to translate the secret texts written in Sanskrit into the popular vernacular. Thus the tradition of mysticism and meditation began within the populace in India.

And how did the various meditative techniques begin? There are some questions which seem to be uppermost in the mind of humankind throughout the ages: who created the universe? How life came on Earth? What is the purpose of life? Why are we born and why do we die? Is there any systematic plan behind all this or is it happening on its own?

In trying to find some clues to these questions there developed two approaches. There were the groups of people who started looking for clues in the outside world. They went on discovering laws of nature, finding its various phenomena, inventing wonderful gadgets, machinery and electronic devices, etc. Their entire research on the external world gave rise to science. Their constant endeavor resulted in unfolding of mysteries behind nature's physical and biological laws. The development in science and technology around us that we see today is the result of the constant endeavor of such people. This ongoing research to unleash the secrets of nature is still going on.

Then there was another group that were of the opinion that if some creator has created this world, then the same creator must have also created them. So, in a way, they should also be a part of this creation. So instead of going deeper into the depth of outside world why not go within themselves and look for some answers there? So they started experimenting on themselves and got involved in inventing various methods for going within. This endeavor of going within gave rise to meditation.

They started researching on their body. They moved their attention inwards and started developing techniques of penetrating deeper into their inner existential identity. All the meditation techniques and yogic exercises are a result of this endeavor taken by millions of those avid curious people who dared to go within.

In their meditative state, these people realized the energy field of consciousness which pervades the whole cosmos. In the deeper state of meditation one realized the omnipresent element of all; the self. In reality what is present everywhere is not energy but pure supreme consciousness which pervades the whole universe.

There are four categories of brain wave patterns. The most rapid is called a beta brain wave pattern, the pattern of normal waking consciousness. Beta is associated with concentration, arousal, alertness, and cognition. At its highest, most rapid levels, though, beta is associated with anxiety, disharmony, and *unease*.

As one becomes more relaxed, one's brain wave activity slows into what is called an alpha brain wave pattern. Alpha patterns vary from deep alpha, a state of deep relaxation often referred to as the twilight state between sleep and waking, to the higher end of alpha which is a more focused yet still very relaxed state.

Slower still are theta waves. Theta is best known as the brain wave state of dreaming sleep, but it is also associated with a number of other beneficial states, including increased creativity, some kinds of superlearning, increased memory abilities, and what are called integrative experiences.

And lastly there are delta waves which are associated with dreamless sleep. These are the slowest brain wave patterns. It is a deep trancelike, nonphysical state with loss of body awareness

Meditation is generally a subjective, personal experience and most often done without any external involvement, except perhaps prayer beads to count prayers. Meditation often involves invoking and cultivating a feeling or internal state, such as compassion, or attending to some focal point, etc. The term can refer to the process of reaching this state, as well as to the state itself.

There are hundreds of specific types of meditation. The word, 'meditation,' means many things dependent upon the context of its use. People practice meditation for many reasons within the context of their culture. Meditation is a component of many religions, and has been practiced since antiquity, especially by monastics.

But how to meditate? Most people live in a world of duality—joy and despair, pleasure and pain, good and evil, love and hatred, richness and poverty, etc. They experience plenty of the negative—despair, pain, evil, hatred, poverty. Yet God created everything. Why would he create all these negative things? An excellent question. God created souls, which have all the qualities of God, including free will. Souls who have "fallen" from the heights of omniscience, omnipotence, etc. have covered the qualities of joy, goodness, etc. with "veils," "mud," "soot" or whatever metaphor you want. Souls created negativity! So instead of pleading with God to remove negativity, they can choose to remove the veils by earnestly seeking God. By communing with God for thousands of hours, they harmonize with Him and "burn" their bad **karma** [kormu (Sanskrit) "deed; cause and effect"], that is, the undesirable results of their free will.

As we rapidly move toward the "shift" you may find that you feel that it is impossible to have enough time to meditate for thousands of hours to achieve the higher consciousness so desired and needed for the New Age that is developing. However, as noted previously, time is speeding up and with time speeding up then it is also possible to learn to meditate and move from one level of achievement to the next level in a much shorter time period. **Karma** will burn faster and the results and achievements of meditation will become known and felt on a much grander scale and more rapidly than ever imagined before.

If you want to use thought to its full potential, you must learn to think consciously apart from the brain. The brain is a wonderful and most useful tool but for most creative work, creation of the highest order, the brain is like a strait-jacket which restricts, binds and limits the action of the mind. So it is necessary to learn to meditate and to go within to find the higher self.

Now that you understand the need to meditate, and are motivated to do so, you need to learn how to meditate, and then actually do it. The wise men of India were the first to discover how to meditate, and have been practicing it continuously to the present day. Therefore, learn from someone who knows these ancient techniques and is proficient at teaching and practicing them. The foundation of the ancient meditative techniques are essential to learning the new techniques which will lead you into the Center of Polarization (the Heart Center) for more advanced meditation and evolving to the higher realms of consciousness.

The instruction for the new technique of the Heart Center meditation will be given later in much detail, as it is essential to understanding the evolvement of humankind's higher consciousness into the paradigm shift.

The sages of India have a secret that is available to everyone. It has been a long, closely-held secret, which few people have discovered, but, once uncovered, could change your life and all the lives around you. It takes some practice to learn a new skill, but once your journey starts, your soul will push you onward, as this is the culmination of deep longing in your soul.

So the soul, which resides deep in you in all of your incarnations (for you have the same soul throughout all of your incarnations), remembers its Creator—God, Divine Mother, whatever name you prefer to use. The soul pulls you in the direction of your search for the truth and knowledge that sets you free.

The soul has an obsession to get back to its Creator. Because of its obsession, it takes over your desires and dreams and you become obsessed with the search of your soul for the Creator. Therefore you could say that you become possessed by the obsession of your soul.

This manifests itself as desire and love for the absolute truth, and nothing less will satisfy the soul. You could spend a lifetime searching, or you could practice the simple skills given in this book, thereby freeing your soul from its temporary body and finding true bliss and ecstasy. Paramhansa Yogananda [Porumhonsu Yōg-un*ondu] referred to **kriya yoga** [krēyu yōgu (Sanskrit) "technique union"] as being the "airplane route" to enlightenment, but I call the skills you are about to learn here the "rocket-ship approach" to enlightenment. So fasten your seat-belt and get ready to have true ecstasy-bliss every day of your life.

Bliss is the feeling of utter joy and contentment, and ecstasy is a state of rapturous delight, a state of sudden, intense feeling. So let's put them both together as the oneness when merging with the Creator and receiving unconditional love from the Creator. This oneness and love have such a strong vibration that it fills every cell and nerve of your body with bliss, love and devotion, radiating love out from your body in the energy field around you. This feeling of the love and bliss become such a craving for more joy until there becomes an explosive (or implosive) merging. Upon this merging the soul rejoices and the body remembers this ecstatic feeling, the long-lasting feeling of bliss, which permeates the body with wisdom and knowledge from ages past. This is the point of enlightenment.

So if your soul desires ecstatic bliss, let's get started on the ride of your life.

Time? Who Needs Time?

We all need time. The very first thing we need to do is arrange our time so that we can get the practice we need to develop our new skills. We cannot learn a new skill without practice. We need 30 minutes in the morning and 30 minutes in either the afternoon or the evening. So each day we need 2 periods of time, consisting of 30 minutes each. That is 1 hour a day.

During these 30-minute periods we are going to learn and practice meditation (**yoga**). We will be developing the skills that will become a habit in our life. We will be retraining our body to accept what our soul has been wanting and desiring. Our soul's wish is about to come true.

I know you have all heard of the monks, sages and **guru**s with their devotees who meditate for 3 hours and longer, and spend their days in a meditative state, but don't fear, we do not need to devote that much time to get to the ecstasy-bliss state or to have that feeling all day.

The reason why we split the time into 2 sessions is that when we meditate, we are going to be raising our vibrations, and this increased state of vibration will stay with us for a period of time—longer for some devotees and shorter for others. So if we have a session in the morning and another session later on in the day we are able to keep the vibration up from one session to the next. Our body also becomes familiar with a certain schedule and expects certain events to occur within certain periods of time. So we are setting and training our body to have a new habit.

It is also very important that all of the steps are done in the proper order. **Do not skip any steps.** Some steps in the process may seem very easy and you may even feel like nothing is happening. However, there is plenty happening within your body that you may not feel right away, but will become evident later on. Also, all of the steps start out in one direction and are built upon as you progress. So if you skip a step you may find later on that you are lost in the process and therefore you will not benefit as quickly as you would have by following all the steps in the correct order. Remember we are on the "rocket-ship approach" to enlightenment and we want to get there as quickly and safely as possible. Later we will learn how to cut down on the time needed for meditation, but for now we need to form the foundation, and foundations always need to be strong.

Step 1: Getting Nowhere Fast (Learning to Sit)

It is very important that we sit and breathe in the proper way. Learning to sit is a process that will develop and become easier and more comfortable with practice. Do not give up, as we cannot achieve ecstasy-bliss without the proper sitting position.

We will be sitting cross-legged **siddhasana** [sid-osunu (Sanskrit) "perfect posture"] and this can be achieved in several steps as we progress. In the cross-legged position bring the heel of the inner foot further under and press against the **perineum** [perin*ēum (Latin and Greek) "around  evacuation"], the diamond-shaped area between the anus and the genital organ. If your heel cannot reach your **perineum**, then place something firm between them to get the pressure placed on the **perineum**. The main objective here is that you must feel the energy **kundalini** [kundul*ēnē (Sanskrit) "coiled serpent"] from the pressure of the heel against the **perineum** or behind the genitals. It may mean that you have to place your heel on the **perineum** and push upwards toward the genital organ. Move the heel very slightly until you are able to feel the slight arousal of energy. If the arousal becomes too intense then you just back off a little. We are only going to be concerned with the one leg and foot at this point. The other leg can be crossed in front at a comfortable position or even left extended out if this is more comfortable. It is the bottom leg we are concerned with at this point.

Note: If you are unable to sit cross-legged and just cannot manage the heel in the **perineum** then you will need something to simulate that process. Suggestions for this are a tennis ball, a bag of rice, a racket ball, or some other object that is not too hard to cause an uncomfortable feeling. In this manner you can sit with your spine straight and the object you are using can be placed under you to simulate the pressure that would have come from the heel.

Since it is necessary to keep the spine straight, it may be helpful for you to sit in this new position on a cushion on the floor with another cushion behind your back for support. Or you could sit in this position on a sofa or easy chair with a cushion behind your back if needed. If you find that you fall asleep during the practice sessions, then a pillow behind your back would be most useful.

The secret here is to experiment with different arrangements to find what is comfortable for you and what makes the energy flow. Since this is crucial to the whole process, I suggest you take your time to find the right position for you. Do not proceed beyond this step until you have found a comfortable sitting position and you have found the right spot to feel the energy.

Now that we have the sitting in order, we will start with the breathing. You will inhale very deeply, expanding the abdomen as you inhale. Inhale deeply all the way up through your lungs until you feel like the air is going to your shoulders. Then hold the breath for as long as is comfortable. Then exhale slowly, allowing the abdomen to pull back in toward your spine. Do not hold the breath for so long that you cannot breathe normally after exhaling. This is not a contest to see how long you can hold your breath. All that is needed is a hesitation between the inhalation and exhalation.

The next step we want to add is the focus on the Third Eye **ajna chakra** [ujnu chukru (Sanskrit) "Third Eye"]. Many of you will have already heard about the Third Eye, but may not know anything beyond that.

The Third Eye is located between the eyebrows on the forehead. It has a universal mythological history. It is the eye of Horus, of Egyptian mysticism; it is the straight poised snake of the Caduceus; it is the horn of the Unicorn; it is the biblical eye of 'If thine eye be single thy whole body shall be full of light' (Matthew 6:22). But above all, the Third Eye is a physical organ of inner vision of which it has been said: 'Our physical eyes look before us seeing neither past nor future, but the Third Eye embraces eternity.'

Raise your eyes to this point and close them, keeping them at this point during the entire exercise **shambhavi** [shombuvē (Sanskrit) "focusing of the Third Eye"] **mudra** [mudr*o (Sanskrit) "spiritual gesture"]. The Third Eye is the seat of the consciousness and is where all the action takes place.

So just practice the sitting and the breathing and the gazing with eyes closed until you have each one of these firmly implanted in your mind. Once you are ready we are now going to put them all together.

Sitting cross-legged with your heel firmly planted underneath you, and focusing your gaze with eyes closed at the Third Eye, take a deep breath from the abdomen all the way up to the shoulders and hold it for a comfortable time period and then exhale. This process is repeated over and over again slowly for 10 minutes.

After the 10-minute period you will say over and over to yourself, very slowly, and with a long, drawn-out pronunciation, the *AUM* **mantra** [muntru (Sanskrit) "speech"].

The single word **AUM** or **OM** is known as the primary seed or the **bija** [bēju (Sanskrit) "seed"] because it contains within it the seed of all other mantras. **AUM** is the primordial sound, the word. The **mantra AUM** is pronounced "Ahhh-uu-mmmmm". Very softly and gently begin to repeat *AUM* mentally in your mind. The sacred sound will naturally, on its own accord, transform into a more unified sound of **OM**, "Ohhhh-mmmm", rather than *AUM*.

The *AUM* **mantra** is repeated in this way for 20 minutes. If you find that your mind starts to wander and thinks about all the problems of the day and other ideas, then when you notice that you are away from the **OM** you just slowly start up with the **OM** again. You may find that in the beginning you will be bringing your focus back to the **OM** many times. This is OK. Eventually your mind will become calm and silent and the **OM** will just fade away with no other intruding thoughts.

ROUTINE: The 10-minute sitting and breathing exercise **pranayama** [pronu-yomu (Sanskrit) "breath-control"] followed by the 20-minute **mantra** meditation. This is done twice daily until you are very comfortable with it and it has become a habit for you.

Once you have achieved that comfy feeling you are ready to move on to the next step.

Step 2: Putting The Pedal To The Metal

We are now going to add some steps to what you have been practicing in order to start moving the energy up and down the spine. We want to move the energy from the **perineum** to the Third Eye and back down again through the central spinal pipeline **sushumna** [sush*umnu (Sanskrit) "ascent"].

So in order to make this happen we are going to flex the anal sphincter muscle and hold it tightly **mula** [mūlu (Sanskrit) "root"] **bandha** [bundu (Sanskrit) "lock"]. As we feel the arousal/energy (**kundalini**) we are going to draw this energy up through the pelvis into the lower belly pulling in the abdomen and continue drawing up the energy through the spinal pipeline all the way up to the top of the spine at the nape of the neck **medulla oblongata** [med*ulu oblaungg*otu (Latin) "long marrow"]. The nape of the neck is the beginning of the brain stem, so when you have drawn the energy to this point you continue to draw it up through the brain toward the Third Eye. All of this drawing up of the energy from the pelvic region to the Third Eye is done on the inhalation breath.

At the same time gently furrow the brow **shambhavi** [som-bovē (Sanskrit) "furrowing of the brow"], feeling as if the brain is being drawn forward into the Third Eye. Keep the eyes closed and raised to the Third Eye throughout the entire exercise, with a slight furrowing of the brow.

We silently chant a **mantra** during this exercise, called **Hong-Sau** [Haung-Sau (Sanskrit) "I am He"]. Chant silently and inwardly **Hong** on the inhalation and **Sau** on the exhalation following the energy as a thin silver thread up the spine to the Third Eye and then back down to the root.

ROUTINE: Sit cross-legged with the anal sphincter flexed and the brow slightly furrowed, and focus on the Third Eye. Inhale with **Hong** and exhale with **Sau**. As you inhale pull the energy up the spine towards the Third Eye and as you exhale relax the anal sphincter and let the energy descend back down the spine to the **perineum**. Repeat this process for 10 minutes. Then follow with 20 minutes of the **OM** mantra.

Continue with this practice until you can readily feel the energy rising and falling in the spinal pipeline and feel comfortable with the steps. Continue until you can keep the anal sphincter muscle flexed throughout the rise and fall of the energy. When this has become your twice-daily habit you may continue with the next step.

Step 3: Adding Fuel To The Fire

Now we are ready to throw more fuel on our internal fires. Continuing with the exercise that is now rapidly becoming an addiction, we are going to turn up the heat some more.

You may wonder why we are focusing so intently on the energy moving up and down the spine. As we go through our incarnations we have created actions (**karma**) in our lives which have caused blockages. These blockages become lodged in our chakras, which are located along the spinal column. In order to reach enlightenment these blockages must be removed. So the process of moving the energy up and down the spine clears the blockages, purifies the chakras, and burns off the **karma** we have created during our incarnations. So let's turn up the heat and burn off some **karma**.

After you get yourself comfortably settled into your 10-minute exercise and the energy is flowing smoothly up and down the spine, we are going to add a chin churn **jalandhara nauli** [jolund*oru noulē (Sanskrit) "chin churn"], which is a neck/head rotation. On the inhalation we fill the lungs with air and slightly sway the head between left and right a few times to get the feeling going and then, making the swaying motion more acute, we swoop down across the chest with the chin and "launch" left, making two complete circles, lifting the head and exhaling. You will feel slightly dizzy, and exhilarated!

Continue in this manner, switching directions of each "launch" until you can work up to about 5 minutes of this action within your 10-minute period.

Once you have this technique integrated in your program you can add the *abdominal pump* **uddiyana nauli** [ūdē*yonu noulē (Sanskrit) "to fly up churn"]). This should follow the chin churn to further move the energy up the spine. Pull in the abdominal muscles on the inhalation, pulling the energy very strongly from the pelvic region upward through the spine to the Third Eye. Then exhale, relaxing the abdomen and, without inhaling, pull your abdomen in toward the spine and pump your abdominal muscles in and out several times. This exercise can be repeated several times to feel that the energy is now flowing very strongly.

If you have a problem getting the hang of the abdominal pumping, it may be useful to practice it during the day standing up (on an empty stomach). Once you get the hang of it standing up, then it is easier to incorporate it into your 10-minute period while sitting.

To practice, stand and place your hands on your knees. Exhale completely and draw the abdomen in as if you feel it is sticking into your spine. Then while it is drawn in and tight, pump it in and out several times. Then relax. Then repeat the drawing in and pumping action.

These 2 techniques of the chin churn and the abdominal pump within your 10-minute exercise increase the flow of energy rapidly and you will feel this flow very strongly. If you happen to feel your energy subsiding a little then you can just repeat these two techniques again while in your 10-minute *breath-control* session.

ROUTINE: So now you have our 10-minute *breath-control* exercise consisting of squeezing the anal sphincter muscle and the furrowing of the brow with the focus on the Third Eye, and moving the energy up the spine with the head rotation and switching direction on the rotation at each inhalation. Then followed by the *abdominal pump* on the exhalation. Keeping the focus always on the Third Eye with the **Hong-Sau** chant in place during all of these exercises. Then after the *breath-control* 10-

minute session you follow with the 20-minute **OM mantra** meditation.

Step 4: Seeing The Light (Yoni Mudra)

So now we are going to add a step between our breathing and meditation practices. After we finish our 10-minute *breath-control* practice and before we start our 20-minute **OM** meditation we are adding **yoni** [yōnē (Sanskrit) "female genitalia"] **kumbhaka** [kumb*uku (Sanskrit) "suspension of breath"] **mudra**. Place the tips of your 2 index fingers close to the outer corner of the closed eyes against the lower lids and then gently push the eyes in and up and to the center toward the Third Eye. Fill the lungs with air and hold. Close the nostrils with the 2 middle fingers. Drop the head down as far as you can on the chest **jalandhara bandha** [jolund*oru bundu (Sanskrit) "chin lock"] and hold your breath in this position for as long as is comfortable. Lift your head to exhale. Then inhale and repeat the process 2 more times.

In summary, you are pushing in and up against your closed eyes while holding your breath with your head resting on your chest and the nostrils pinched closed with the middle fingers. You should do this 3 times and when you feel comfortable with it and you feel you want to experience more, then you can increase it up to 5 times.

The lights you see will eventually form into what is known as the spiritual eye. It is a dark color in space surrounded by a glittering gold circle with a star in the center of the indigo. The circle and star will begin to sparkle and pulsate and have electrical-looking flashes going throughout 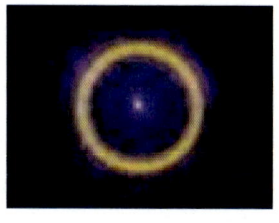 it. The circle of gold will give the impression of the beginning of a tunnel leading to the star in the center. This is a very soothing feeling and the soul loves it and wants more and more of it.

During this exercise you can dwell upon the spiritual eye and feel filled with love and longing for more. But do not try to force this mental image to last during our **OM** meditation. Have comfort in the joy that it gives you and carry that feeling into your meditation.

After this practice you continue straight into the 20-minute **OM** meditation.

Step 5: Reaping Some Benefits (Yoga Sutras)

We have learned a lot now and are well into our daily practices so it is time that we start putting in some requests and reaping the benefits of all our new-found skills. We are now going to string some words together **sutra**s [sūtru (Sanskrit) "stitch"] that will add power and meaning to our meditation.

In order to accomplish this we are now going to advance to a more prolonged meditation.

Our 10-minute *breath-control* meditation will now become a 20-minute *breath-control* meditation. And our 20-minute **OM** meditation becomes 40 minutes. So we have doubled in time on all of our sessions.

During the 40-minute **OM** meditation we start out as usual with the **OM** mantra. Let the **OM mantra** continue until close to the end of your 40-minute period and let the **mantra** become fuzzy and fade into the background of nothingness **samyama** [sum-yomu (Sanskrit) "together control"]. Do not rush **samyama**; it can come at the end of your **OM** meditation. At this point we are going to pick up on the string of words. Always do the same words, in the same order. After a period of time you will notice that these words have changed you and your life.

Pick up each word, one at a time, beginning with LOVE. See the word come into existence and note it mentally by repeating it in you mind only one time, LOVE, and then let it fade into infinity. After a few seconds or even a minute later pick the same word up again, LOVE, and repeat it mentally again

and let it fade into infinity. Start with just 2 mental images of LOVE and work up to 4 times.

Then add another word from the thread into your meditation. The next word is RADIANCE. Again pick up the word from nothingness and repeat it mentally and then let it fade into infinity. Wait a few seconds or even a minute and pick up RADIANCE again. Start with just 2 mental images of RADIANCE and work up to 4 times.

The next word we add to the *stitches* is UNITY. Pick up the word from nothingness and repeat it mentally and then let it go back into infinity. Mentally say the word and again after a few seconds or a minute and let it go again into infinity. Keep the same pattern as the other impressions before this one. Do the mental image at least twice and work up to 4 times.

All the *stitches* should be done the same number of times. So if you start LOVE with 2 times then you need to continue with the remaining *stitches* 2 times. If you are able to do LOVE 4 times then the remaining *stitches* should also be done 4 times.

Continue adding to the *stitches* with the following in the order given:

HEALTH　　　　　　　　　　STRENGTH

ABUNDANCE   PROSPERITY   WISDOM

AKASHA [UK*OSHU] "INNER SPACE"
(Lighter than Air)

SAMYAMA
(Inner Silence)

When you are finished with your *stitches* you then dwell upon the last **sutra**, until the end of the 40-minute meditation session, or if your **sutra**s are following your meditation session then you can continue with the last **sutra** for a little while longer if you desire to do so. If you are unable to continue at any period of time with the **sutra** then switch back to the **OM mantra** for either the duration of the meditation or until you feel you can pick up the **sutra** again.

If you find that you want to add a **sutra** for your particular needs then you should consider carefully what it is you want to add. This is not a section where you use a **sutra** to ask for more money or a better job or some other material aspect that you wish to have in your life. If you are looking for a **sutra** to add that will enhance your spirituality then this is acceptable. Some suggestions that may help you could be: SPIRIT GUIDES, ASCENDED MASTERS, and COMMUNICATION.

You should choose your word or words carefully and be prepared to settle in for the long haul with any **sutra**. A **sutra** is not a word that you put out into the universe for a week or two and then choose another one. These are *stitches* that will be used in your meditation for a very long time. These *stitches* may be in your meditation for many years.

The placement of your **sutra** should be immediately preceding the **akasha sutra**.

ROUTINE: 20-minute *breath-control* with 40-minute **OM** meditation encompassing the **sutra**s in the beginning of the meditation. When you choose to do your **sutra**s at the beginning of the meditation then you will be using **samyama** to lead you into the **OM** meditation.

Karma Yoga

The term **karma yoga** is used frequently and we need to understand its meaning and purpose. In order to properly discuss **karma yoga** we need also to understand **pranayama**.

We have a routine for **pranayama** in our daily meditation practice which encompasses a breathing technique which moves the **kundalini** energy up and down the spinal column between the root chakra and the Third Eye.

By practicing this method we are preparing ourselves for a more advanced technique known as **kriya yoga**. It is preparing us for the stillness of the breath which is necessary to achieve the constant union of the infinite soul.

Kevala [kāvulu (Sanskrit) "absolute"] **kumbhaka** can be achieved and is attainable by practicing **pranayama**. *ABC of Yoga*[7] gives a definition of "**kevala kumbhaka** (perfectly peaceful pause) involves not only complete cessation of movement of air and muscles, but also the awareness of all such movements and tendencies. The state experienced is one [of] complete rest."

Now let's take a look at some definitions of **karma yoga**.

Swami Vivekananda says:

> This world's wheel within wheel is a terrible mechanism; if we put our hands in it, as soon as we are caught we are gone. We all think that when we have done a certain duty, we shall be at rest; but before we have done a part of that duty, another is already in waiting. We are all being dragged along

---

7 ABC of Yoga: http://www.abc-of-yoga.com

by this mighty, complex world-machine. There are only two ways out of it; one is to give up all concern with the machine, to let it go and stand aside, to give up our desires. That is very easy to say, but is almost impossible to do. I do not know whether in twenty millions of men one can do that. The other way is to plunge into the world and learn the secret of work, and that is the way of **karma yoga**. Do not fly away from the wheels of the world-machine, but stand inside it and learn the secret of work. Through proper work done inside, it is also possible to come out. Through this machinery itself is the way out.

We have now seen what work is. It is a part of nature's foundation and goes on always. Those that believe in God understand this better, because they know that God is not such an incapable being as will need our help. Although this universe will go on always, our goal is freedom, our goal is unselfishness; and according to **karma yoga**, that goal is to be reached through work."

This is the generally accepted definition of **karma yoga**. That of giving oneself to work or service without expecting anything in return. In other words the doing of work as a service from our generosity and love for God.

However a quote from Lahiri Mahasaya puts a different perspective on **karma yoga** in his explanation of *Gita* 4:21:

"This verse denotes that the one who practices **kevala** named action through this body becomes passive, is engrossed in the soul and relinquishes all the sensory propensities, is devoid of sin.

"Thus it can be clearly understood that God has termed that **kevala karma** to be the true **karma yoga**. Elsewhere God has stated this action to be **sahaja** [suh*oju (Sanskrit) "natural"] **karma**. Therefore what is **kevala karma** is **sahaja karma** and this is **karma yoga**. God through the medium of Arjuna has advised humankind to follow this **karma yoga**.

So what does this mean for us? It is necessary to give love unto the world and humankind from the goodness of our hearts and in return we will receive love. However, it does not mean that you have to go and slave away for a religious organization in hopes that you will receive salvation in return. It does not work that way. If you feel good about giving of your time and service and wish to give a day every now and then and do it with love, expecting nothing in return, then this is a proper attitude and you should proceed. However if you feel obligated to give your service voluntarily, day in and day out, and think that you are going to receive salvation in return, then you are wasting your time. God knows whether you have the right attitude in your heart.

Organizations that charge fees, or even ask for donations, for their ashrams, temples, or **yoga** (meditation) instruction are not giving of themselves in a godly way. God does not charge fees for his love and you should not have to pay for learning how to love and receive God.

This means giving of your self in hard labor, as well. Many organizations or institutions will ask that you pay to visit with them and request that you do service while you are there as your **karma yoga** and service for God. This is not the proper attitude and you should never have to pay in money or service to any organization or institution that is giving instruction. This is why Mahavatar Babaji prohibited the idea of forming organizations. If a disciple forms an organization he then becomes obligated to the administration of that organization for which he has formed and must raise money for various buildings which he may wish to erect and various programs he wishes to put into practice.

By then becoming bogged down in the administration of an organization he allows the ego to creep back in and is involved in the daily operation and function of the organization itself.

It is necessary to devote oneself to the meditation technique and the search of the inner silence of God within. For this you do not need to give labor or money.

Step 6: The Big Secret (Kriya Yoga)

The history of **kriya yoga** dates back to ancient India. **Kriya yoga** meditation is perhaps one of the oldest types of meditation techniques in the world. It is in the ***Bhagavad Gita*** that one first finds the reference to **kriya yoga** by Lord Krishna. Besides, this branch of **yoga** has also been mentioned by **Patanjali** (Put*unjulē) in his ***Yoga Sutras***. In the second chapter of the ***Yoga Sutras***, he explains the concept of **kriya yoga**. **Kriya** refers to action. **Kriya yoga**, thus, is the **yoga** of action.

It has been mentioned time and again that **kriya yoga** was once practiced extensively in ancient India. With time, however, the techniques of this **yoga** were lost. The primary reason for this was that **kriya yoga** was practiced by the sages. These hermits passed on the knowledge only to their disciples but kept it away from the reach of ordinary men. Lahiri Mahasaya received the knowledge of **kriya yoga** by the immortal Yogi Mahavatar Babaji in 1861, which is recounted in Paramhansa Yogananda's autobiography. Yogananda wrote that Mahavatar Babaji told Lahiri Mahasaya "The **kriya yoga** that I am giving to the world through you in this nineteenth century, is a revival of the same science that Krishna gave millenniums ago to Arjuna and was later known to **Patanjali** and to Christ, St. John, St. Paul, and other disciples."

We are now going to learn a technique that for thousands of years has been made available directly only from **guru** to disciple and to only a chosen few. This technique is known as **kriya yoga** and is a technique that we will incorporate into our 20-minute *breath-control* session. **Kriya** is a technique which has many stages and like any other learning process we will begin with stage 1.

To begin with, we sit in our cross-legged (**siddhasana**) position with spine straight, but relaxed, and our heel in the proper position to feel the **kundalini** energy.

Very slightly flex or squeeze the epiglottis, a membrane attached to the root of the tongue, to enhance the process of incoming air and breathe in deeply, drawing the energy up the spine and consciously direct the flow of incoming air across the spot where it enters the nasal passage from the throat, which is at the root of the palate. This technique is done with the mouth closed although it may be easier to learn the process with the mouth open. So it is OK if you need to practice a few minutes with the mouth open in order to understand how this process is working. The air will feel cool as it passes this sensitive spot and will make a slightly audible vibration. Restrict the flow of air through the larynx, producing a "just audible" snoring sound. No nasal sound should be heard. As the throat passage is narrowed, the airway is narrowed, creating such a "rushing" sound. And be sure that you have your focus on the Third Eye at all times and to continue with **Hong Sau**. Continue the inhalation and drawing of **kundalini** up toward the Third Eye.

Now there are some additional points that can be added to the method above to make it even more effective. You breathe in and out very, very gently, without making a sound, ideally, or next to no sound. The one sensory feedback you have, is the faint feeling of cool air in the throat, maybe a muffled vibration there too. Yet the breath itself is soundless, and so effortless that it would not move a feather held in front of the face.

Do not tense your eyes, neck, nostrils, jaws, and root of the tongue, and do not hoist your shoulders either. But try to put the tongue somewhere further back in the mouth while you are at it, place the tongue at that point on the top of the mouth where the soft and hard palate meet. Alternatively, bend the tongue back so that the tip of the tongue presses the back of the soft palate on the roof of the mouth without strain. Some say you should lift the tip of your tongue to get twice the effect of the breathing practice, but if you just "make it thick" and draw it backwards somewhat, it may work a little better, along with the inaudible breathing. Do not breathe jerkily or irregularly in this exercise, but let the breathing movements be smooth, steady and continuous.

As you are drawing the **kundalini** upwards, be sure to follow the energy flow from the root or **perineum** up through the **sushumna** to the **medulla oblongata**. The **sushumna** is your spinal pipeline and is a very dark tunnel until you fill it with the light and energy of the **kundalini**. So follow this light all the way from the root to the **medulla oblongata** and upward to the Third Eye during the inhalation of **kriya**. The inhalation is cooling to the body. Then on the reverse follow the light and energy as it descends from the Third Eye back down the **sushumna** to the root on the exhalation of the **kriya**. The exhalation is warming to the body.

As you become more comfortable with **kriya** you can start to flex or squeeze the epiglottis more tightly on the exhalation, so that you have a partial closure of the epiglottis on the inhalation and a more pronounced closure of the epiglottis on the exhalation.

The position of the hands should be relaxed with palms up, resting either on the knee portion of the crossed legs or beside the crossed-legs. The index finger should form a circle by touching the thumb. This hand position should be held throughout the sittings in meditation.

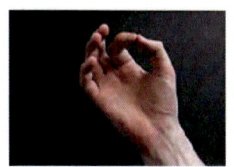

ROUTINE: Our 20-minute *breath-control* exercise will now consist of the **kriya** technique for breathing instead of just the normal inhalation and exhalation. Everything else in this exercise remains the same.

This is a very powerful technique and you will begin to feel more energy flowing up and down the **sushumna**. Then follow with the 40-minute meditation, including the **sutra**s.

Step 7: Fanning The Flames

We are now going to concentrate again on the 20-minute *breath-control* period and add another technique onto our **kriya**. It is the technique known as **kechari** (kāchur*ē (Sanskrit) "flying through inner space") **mudra** and like **kriya** it comes in stages. We will start with stage 1. Stage 1 of **kechari mudra** is to place the tip of the tongue at the top of the mouth where the soft palate meets the hard palate. Rub this upper portion of the palate with the tip of the tongue in order to excite the nerves in the upper mouth.

Then just make the tongue a little thick and draw it backwards a little and place it over this portion of the upper mouth where the soft and hard palate meet. You should draw down a bit on this thick part of the tongue so that you feel as though you are sucking on something in your mouth.

The tongue is held in this position during all the techniques that you are performing during **pranayama**.

There is just one more technique that should be addressed here before we move on. During the **yoni mudra** you have been raising the head to exhale and inhale. If you have advanced enough in your techniques that you are seeing the spiritual eye clearly during the **yoni mudra** and if you have worked up to 5 repetitions then it is desirable to modify this technique just a little. The modification will consist of the elimination of the lifting of the head during exhalation and inhalation. You will merely release the middle fingers to exhale and inhale without lifting the head and replace the middle fingers to continue on with the practice. In this way you are keeping your attention on the star within the spiritual eye at all times. You may increase the time of this technique to 5 minutes.

It is also desirous to be closing off the ear canal during this technique so rather than use the traditional method of the thumbs I suggest that you get some earplugs and use them while you are meditating. It is a simple and effective method.

ROUTINE: In summary, following your *breath-control* session of 20 minutes is the **yoni mudra** which is then followed by the 40-minute meditation consisting of the *stitches* at the beginning of the meditation.

Step 8: Got Rhythm? (Navi Kriya)

By this time you are well into deep meditation and your *breath-control* techniques have become an easy habit. We are going to add a technique called **navi** [novē (Sanskrit) "navel" and "boat"] **kriya**. I look upon it more as a rhythm than a technique, as this technique actually sets a rhythm to your *breath-control* and meditation. We will add **navi kriya** in a couple of steps.

Navi kriya has to do with the navel. So to begin with we will place it in the 20-minute session of the meditation. To perform **navi kriya** you pull the navel (belly button) inward toward the spine on the inhalation and then roll upward with the diaphragm. You will feel as though you are pulling up behind the heart. This actually becomes a rhythmic motion of pulling inward and upward. On the exhalation the stomach will be slightly pushed forward, as it is the reverse of the inward and upward action. On the pulling in and up you will also be pulling a slight flow of energy up to the Third Eye. You will need to hold the breath momentarily at the Third Eye before starting the exhalation. The breath is very shallow, almost nonexistent. If you breathe deeply you will hyperventilate, get dizzy and possibly pass out.

This is a gentle action, like the rolling of a boat on a wave, as actually that is what **navi** means, "boat"; and that is why it is mostly just getting into a rhythm. Be sure that you are still inwardly chanting your **Hong Sau**—**Hong** *o*n the inhalation and **Sau** on the exhalation.

This rhythm is performed in conjunction with your stage 1 **kriya yoga** breathing technique and the stage 1 **kechari mudra**. Remember that you are still squeezing the anal sphincter muscle, holding it tightly (root lock) and focusing on the Third Eye. To add more energy to this technique you can modify the rhythm every once in a while to hold the energy on the inhalation at the Third Eye for 1-5 seconds. Do this a few times every once in a while to increase the energy level.

ROUTINE: In summary, your *breath-control* session of 20 minutes now consists of the neck/head rotation, *chin churn* followed by the *abdominal pump* and then followed by **navi kriya** rhythm at the same time as stage 1 **kechari mudra** which, you will remember, is the lifting of the tongue to the top of the mouth and pressing back as far back as you can with the tongue, and using the **kriya** breathing technique. Then at the end of your *breath-control* session is the **yoni mudra,** which is then followed by the 40-minute **OM** meditation, which includes the **sutra**s. At all times now in the mediation session you will use the **navi kriya** rhythm in your breathing technique along with the **kriya** breathing technique.

Yogic Sleeping & Protection

By now we have covered a lot of ground, but we have not covered anything to do with sleeping and what our minds are doing at night. We have learned to go deeply into meditation, we have learned to raise the **kundalini** and open the Third Eye. We are well on our way to self-realization.

We are now going to incorporate our **sutra**s into what is called **yoga nidra** [nēdru (Sanskrit) "sleep"]. **Yoga nidra** is yogic sleeping. There are many programs available in this country calling themselves **yoga nidra**. There are guided meditations, the law of attraction, programs whereby you can visualize and have affirmations to receive whatever you desire in life. These are NOT **yoga nidra**. **Yoga nidra** is an ancient technique and is a guided meditation of sorts for the purpose of training the mind to go inward and become subtler and subtler until the attention goes off into stillness.

Yoga nidra is a state of consciousness, not a method.

So we will use a set of **sutra**s as the method to obtain **yoga nidra**. We will use the **sutra**s the same way as we have been all along, that is, picking up a **sutra** and mentally saying it and letting it fall away for around 15 seconds or more and then picking it up again and repeating it again.

We will do this in bed at the time that we are retiring for the night. You will need some ear plugs, the kind that swimmers use, as these are of durable plastic and seal off the ear canal better than the foam plugs.

So when you are ready to go to bed, put in the ear plugs and lie on your back in the bed with a pillow under your head. Close your eyes and begin to pick up the **sutra**s in the following order one at a time:

FEET

STARS

MOON

SUN

SOLAR SYSTEM

GALAXY

COSMOS

UNITY

It will be OK if you fall asleep. If you then awake and find that you did not complete the **sutra**s, then you can pick up where you left off. It is OK to fall asleep again.

You will find the next morning that it is not the same kind of sleep you normally have. This is a deep sleep, a yogic sleep (**yoga nidra**). It is a fully conscious state of deep sleep.

You may also find that when you first start with the ear plugs that you are hearing body sounds such as your heart beat and the blood rushing through the veins. This will subside with persistence.

After doing this for several sessions you will begin to feel more of the cosmos around you and begin to feel unity. You will be able to examine your thoughts while in yogic sleep as though they were playing out on a stage.

Make yogic sleep a part of your routine. Do it every night. Even if you are tired and fall asleep after the first **sutra** you will still be accomplishing something. And we all know that something is better than nothing.

The ear plugs are serving a different purpose, but it is an easy way to accomplish the mastering of the **AUM** sounds. By wearing earplugs for a very long period of time you will eventually feel and hear the *AUM*. This could happen at any time of the day or night, sleeping or awake, in meditation or not in meditation. It is a very melodious sound of the prolonged, never ending sound of the word **AUM**. The ear plug method is an easy way of achieving this with no effort on your part.

Actually this whole step of yogic sleeping requires very little effort on your part, but in conjunction with all the other techniques you will notice some rapid progress.

Let's now look at adding some protection to ourselves which can be accomplished when first awaking in the mornings it is always a good idea to place a protective field around you. A protective field is like a science fiction force field. It is a field of light and surrounds you like a bubble.

In order to accomplish this upon first waking, you will rest still and comfortably and imagine a bright light like the sun shining down upon your body. You will say to yourself mentally:

"The light is very bright, the brightest light you have ever seen. It is surrounding my body with love and light. It is so bright, white bright, I can feel the warmth surrounding my body. It is starting at the feet and I feel the warmth moving up my body to my head. I am surrounded by the white light of love and protection."

The words do not have to be exactly as above but you can say them in your own way to give your unconscious mind the affirmation of the protection. Several times during the day you should repeat the visualization of the light surrounding your body and remind yourself that you are protected by the white light of love and protection.

Step 9: Contemplating the Navel

By now you are well into your practice of the **navi kriya** rhythm, so we will add the remaining steps to this technique.

In order to properly and successfully perform **navi kriya** you will need to make yourself a string of beads. **Mala** [molu (Sanskrit) "garland"] beads typically come in a length of 108 beads with 1 extra bead, the turning bead, to mark the end of the counting rotation. **Mala** beads are used for counting sacred mantras and chants.

However, since we cannot get **mala** beads in the correct length for the **navi kriya** we will need to make our own string of beads. If you are able to count the cycles on your hand then this is preferable to a string of beads. However for those of you who have not learned the counting technique then beads are the way to go for now. You will need to make a string of beads. Pop beads, also known as Pop-It beads, Pop-Together beads, Snap beads, and Snap-Together beads, work best. Make a string of 25 beads, then follow with a large washer. Then add 100 more beads and follow with another large washer. Pop the beads together finishing in a circle like a necklace. The beads are held in the right hand over the third finger and the thumb is used to pull the bead toward you as you perform the **navi kriya** counts.

The breathing in **navi kriya** is most important. For **navi kriya** you will drop the head forward and rest the chin on your chest. Be sure that your eyes are closed and that the eyes are positioned upward on the Third Eye on both the inhalation and the exhalation. The inhalation and the exhalation are accomplished with the **kriya** breathing technique that you have already learned. Using your beads to count, you will perform **navi kriya** for 100 (half) **OM** counts with the head down, that is, **OM** on inhalation and **OM** on exhalation. That makes 2 (half) counts, 2 beads. Every time you chant **OM** you pull a bead toward you for the count. Then raise the head and tilt it backwards and perform in this position for 25 (half) **OM** counts. You will then repeat the cycle again so that you are starting with 3 complete cycles of **navi kriya**. This is a very powerful technique. You will be working up to 4 complete **navi kriya** cycles in this session.

Again, to have a more pronounced energy level, you can modify the rhythm every once in a while to hold the energy at the Third Eye for 1-5 seconds. Do this every once in a while when you feel you can handle more energy. It will continually raise the energy just a little more each time. Eventually you will notice that you are high and buzzing with energy and vibrations. You have accomplished this with no drugs and no alcohol. You can keep this energy going throughout the meditation and a portion of this energy will stay with you, but you need to replenish it by meditating twice daily to "stay high."

On the inhalation you will be pulling inward at the navel, as if you are breathing in through the navel, and as you inhale you will catch up the **kundalini** that is rising from the root to join with the breath from the navel, and the 2 joined together will proceed up the spinal column to the Third Eye.

This method of moving the energy is very important and you will feel as though you are breathing from the navel. Again you may increase the energy level by holding the breath on the Third Eye before starting the downward flow of the energy back to the root. The flow of energy being swept up with the **kriya** breathing is most important.

This is not a technique where you need to hold your breath and take so long to move the energy upward that you are out of breath. That is not the idea. The breathing should be in the rhythm of the rocking boat. Because the breath is quite fast it should be shallow. If it is deep you will hyperventilate. If you pause at the end of the inhalation and again pause at the end of the exhalation you will be teaching your breath to extend itself naturally and you may even find that eventually the breath stops on its own.

Most people will be able to identify more with swinging on a swing than rocking in a boat. It's easy to imagine yourself on a swing, going up and back, and down and forward. Pleasant memories of childhood should make this a fun exercise. Slipping through both space and time may raise your consciousness. Bliss is creeping up on you!

Radha and Krishna on a swing

A more aggressive attitude may yield imagines of a battering ram, suspended from a wooden frame, knocking down the gates of heaven!

If you find that you are having a problem continuing with the cycles because you keep slipping into the inner silence then we allow the inner silence to take precedence.

Your time for meditation has now been extended and you have progressed to the point where you no longer need to keep track of the time for any of your meditation sessions.

ROUTINE:
Pranayama (20-minute session)
Chin churn (**jalandhara mudra**)
Abdominal Pump
With **Hong-Sau** (**Hong** on inhalation and **Sau** on exhalation)
With **kriya** breathing technique
With tongue pressed upward and back (**Khechari mudra**)
With the mouth closed and silently chanting
With flexing of the anal sphincter (**mulabandha***)*
With focusing on the Third Eye (**shambhavi mudra***)*
With the rhythm of the rocking boat (**navi kriya**)
Then do **yoni mudra**
Deep Meditation (70-minute session)
3 cycles of **navi kriya OM** counts
Then follow with the **sutra**s
    Then follow with deep meditation of **OM**
    Keep the energy rising and falling
    Focus on the Third Eye
    Use **kriya** breathing
    Inwardly chant **OM** on the inhalation and **OM** on the exhalation
    (moving towards 1 long **OM** on the exhalation only.
    Move towards the stillness inside.
    Meditate upon the nothingness and silence within.

Merits and Demerits of Spiritual Organizations

If spiritual organizations are for beginner souls then we need to question the purposes of spiritual organizations and the churches of the various religions. Once a soul joins a church he thinks he will be taught the ways of God. But will he really be taught about God, or the way of God, or the way to get to God?

A soul will not learn in a church what he needs to find his way back to God because most people who join religious organizations are involved in the churches for friendship and fellowship. Most churches will even advertize along the "Fellowship" lines. This is not teaching the soul how to find its way back to God. If a person stays in a religious organization, then he will become dependant upon it and is not secure within himself to step out and find his own spiritual path.

Remember that in the beginning of this book we pointed out that your soul has an obsession to get back to its Creator. Because of its obsession, it takes over your desires and dreams. This longing of the soul is an individual development and must be sought by the individual. You cannot be led to salvation by a preacher or priest. The way to salvation is through meditation. And meditation will be hampered if the individual remains in a spiritual organization.

You may ask why is this so? All of my friends belong to this church. Well, that is just the problem. The way to God is a private and lonely path and must be found between you and God. If the leaders of your church are not meditating, then they have not found their way to God either. How can they lead you to God if they have not found God? They say you should just accept Jesus as your saviour and you will be saved. This is not finding God! Even Jesus withdrew into the desert to fast and meditate.

Meditation is a private affair and is for the purpose of spiritual development. You will not advance spiritually unless you are able to withdraw into your own self and find your own pathway to God and enlightenment. The teachings of spiritual organizations are not conducive to this way of life and therefore become only a hindrance in the advancement of one's spiritual path.

Jesus did not teach his disciples to become members of spiritual organizations. Instead he taught them to meditate and showed them the way to finding the truth within themselves.

Because you are reading this you are obviously beyond the point of being a beginner soul. So now it is time for you to grow up and further your spiritual development.

There have been some mystics within the spiritual organizations but these mystics have basically just been tolerated by the organizations, as this is not something that the organization would want to advertize and teach to all of their members.

[The following section is by Swami Satyeswarananda Giri Babaji Mahraj[8]. He has been associated with Paramhansa Yogananda and Swami Sri Yukteswar. The great yogi Babaji sent this swami to America to reestablish kriya, and has lived in San Diego ever since.]

The emotional and devotional seekers of Truth think that if they join a spiritual group, organization or hermitage, this will expedite their spiritual growth, or help them to make quick progression in their spiritual endeavors. These feelings in them are natural and normal.

---

[8] http://www.sanskritclassics.com/organizations1.htm

But when they actually join an organization, they find out that a lot of work is involved, and, contrary to their expectations, they do not have enough time to meditate.

This is not the mere logical deduction, inference or intellectual speculation of the author, who himself had direct experience in his young days studying and living with others in a hermitage (without joining formally and officially), and who witnessed and experienced firsthand what organizations could offer.

During the devotional seekers' sojourn in the hermitage, they find themselves in an uncomfortable situation, having no time for actual meditation, and they become disillusioned. At this point, the honest seekers will leave the organization and seek out the right lifestyle to pursue the spiritual path.

Some seekers develop interest in name and fame and hang around the organization for a while. They engage in a play of power and, if they lose, then they split from the main organization and start their own new organization and become the head.

Others stay on in the organization, as they have established an easygoing lifestyle and are afraid to venture out. They are haunted by feelings of insecurity and are so weak that they cannot consider leaving their secure way of life together with the other hermits.

The organized way of religious groups provides an opportunity for the general public to promote their religious life in society, apparently. Society has developed this notion that living in the spiritual communities or organizations will enhance their spiritual progress.

> In fact, the spiritual organizations are nothing but Kindergarten schools for novices on the spiritual path.

The organized way of religion, the very idea itself, originates from confusion, and the seeker is tricked by the mind in a subtle way. Mind is the Satan, and mind plays subtle tricks on the seeker of Truth who wants to join a hermitage for a better lifestyle, imagining this will help him make progress.

> "Nobody is a sinner, or Satan. Only the mind is Satan ... " *Lahiri Mahasay's Personal Letters to Kriya Disciples*, The Sanskrit Classics, 1985, Letter number 68.

The idea of living together in a better lifestyle is very palatable from the human point of view. This idea tricks the seeker in a subtle way to lean, or depend, on quantitative and collective improvement of spirituality in society, but this improves neither the quality of the peoples' individual lives nor their collective life. The organized way of religions neither helps individuals to improve the quality of life, nor does it improve society in general.

On the other hand, *Guru-param-para*, or the personal relationship between Master and disciple and learning from the Master (as opposed to learning from an organization), enables the seeker to find the righteous way to make himself inward and dissolve the mind in the very Source, where he thus attains purification of his heart. The disciple then sees perfection in the manifested world, or society, and he sees the Lord in every manifestation. As the seeker sees the Lord everywhere, the quality of his life is thus improved, and he does not bother others whose time is not ripe.

Organized religious groups send their agents to society to preach to people whose time is not ripe, unsettling their minds and creating more confusion in them. To speak truthfully, the people's providence triumphs. They simply are not able to understand such theoretical preaching, and the words of the so-called spiritual leaders are not effective because when their preaching strikes the providence of others, it becomes fragmented.

The realized Masters restrain themselves and do not bother to unsettle the minds of the people, but rather effectively help the seekers whose time is ripe. They keep themselves inward and enjoy the Tranquility in Oneness. Here, the *Guru-Param-Para* way, being the righteous way, helps the seeker to dissolve the sophisticated tricks of the mind and dissolves the negative aspect of individuality, thereby pointing to the qualitative aspect of life.

Joining organized religious groups and allowing oneself to be involved in an apparent renunciate life points to the quantitative aspect. Through the quantitative way, people never achieve the qualitative way. Only by dissolving the mind in its Source and being in Oneness with the pure Consciousness does the seeker attain the infinite Consciousness qualitatively and quantitatively as well.

So, in regards to the matter of spiritual progression, we must approach the subject of organized religious groups and organizations very carefully. It is very important to find the righteous way, and yet this way is rarely found.

In the *Bhagavad Gita* 4:1-2, [t]he verses say, I [Lord Krisna] had instructed this message of *yoga* to the Sun [Sun-God], who related it to his son Manu [the father of Humankind]. Manu told this to Ikkhaku, and thus according to the personal relations of *Guru-param-para* [considered to be the righteous way], the message was received, or taught.

In the course of time, the personal relationship was broken, and the eternal message lost its proper perspective. Thus, I have revived it and tell you [Arjuna].

Hence, according to the holy Scripture, *Guru-param-para* is the righteous way, and organized institutionalization is the negative force which attempts to break this proper chain of successions of personal relationships between Master and disciples and to bypass the righteous way.

Organized religious institutions of Hinduism, Buddhism, Judaism, Christianity and Islam and all other groups of organized religion — bypass this righteous way.

In the name of religious institutions to promote the cause of religions among the people in society, a group of persons start spiritual organizations as non-profit, and they invite donations. At the appropriate time, or season, the authorities of these organizations send out their agents to collect tax-deductible donations to enhance their security in the name of serving society. Moreover, the religious organization, being "non-profit," does not have to pay a tax on the amount collected. Neither does the donor have to pay a tax. Yet it is not uncommon for the religious organization to turn around and use the donations for income-producing investments.

The hermits pollute not only themselves through these donations but also pollute the householders who donate. Regardless of the character of the donation, both the donor and donee are involved in collusion, in a strict spiritual sense.

"And Jesus went into the temple of God, and cast out all them that sold and bought in the temple, and overthrew the table of the money changers, and the seats of them that sold doves." Matt. 21:12

"And said to them, It is written, my house shall be called the house of prayer; but ye have made it a den of thieves." Matt. 21:13

To speak the truth, in the language of the great ancient Yogi Patanjali, *Asteya* means not to steal under any circumstances. Allowing oneself to be involved in the collection of donations on behalf of non-profit organizations, in the strict and subtle spiritual sense, amounts to stealing from the donors. And, as such, in the spiritual light, it is an act of connivance which pollutes both the hermits and the donors.

Similarly, *Aparigraha*, that is, help or donations from others without unconditional love and affection, but rather conditional with attachment, desires and expectations of getting something in return (for example, tax deductions, being healed from physical, mental and spiritual ailments, obtaining a lucrative position, or any favor whatsoever, including winnings from lawsuits), pollutes the receivers of such donations. As a result, they cannot improve their lot on the spiritual path. So the effect of the donor's cause goes to the receivers of the donations, the hermits or renunciates, and contaminates them, regardless of what they practice.

> In the *Yoga Sutras* 2:32, [t]he verse says, *Socha* (Purity in body and mind), *Santosh* (Contentment of heart), *Tapa* (Austerities), *Swadhyaya* (Self-study, or self-analysis) and *Iswar-pranidhanani* (Surrendering to the inner Lord) are the spiritual rules, the other five Commandments, which formulate the second step according to Yogi Patanjali, the founding father of *Raja* Yoga.

The seeker might remember that the Holy Bible spoke, in the same spirit, of ten Commandments to practice and observe, for attaining inner Realization of the ultimate Self.

The subtle point is that the hermits are already tempted by the subtle tricks of the mind to find better security in organized religious groups. The lifestyle maintained through such polluted donations prevents the hermits from improving their situation. They simply fail to perceive it, as they are in a confused and/or complacent state of mind and are terrified of losing their security in their old age.

Accepting donations does not affect the realized yogi, who never sees anyone except the ultimate Self. Advanced yogis sometimes do accept donations under certain circumstances in order to keep harmony, but they do not accept these for personal use, and thus they remain free from pollution. They simply give away such donations to some needy people.

Let us see what the Bible has to say about this point again:

> "No man can serve two masters: for either he will hate the one [Inwardness or Detachment], and love the other [Outwardness or Attachment]; or else he will hold to the one, and despise the other." *Matt.*6:24
>
> "For where your treasure is, there will your heart be also." *Matt.* 6:21
>
> "Take therefore no thought for the morrow: for the morrow shall take thought for the things of itself." *Matt.* 6:34

The above particular verse reminds us of the wandering mendicant of Vedic culture, who does not save his alms for tomorrow. At noontime, by rule, he can beg for alms from three to seven doors from outside uttering, *Bhabati bhikhang dehi*, that is, "Please give alms."

If he does not find his prepared food at the stipulated doors, then he is supposed to return to his niche and drink water from nature and consider that the lot of providence has not offered him food today and pray for himself as well as for the world.

> "Behold the fowls of the air: for they sow not, neither do they reap, nor gather into barns; yet your heavenly Father feedeth them. Are ye not much better than they?" Matt. 6:26
>
> "Which of you by taking thought can add one cubit unto his stature?" "And why take ye thought for raiment? Consider the lilies of the field, how they grow; they toil not, neither do they spin." Matt. 6:27-28
>
> "Wherefore, if God so clothe the grass of the field, which today is, and tomorrow is cast into the oven, shall he not much more clothe you, O ye of little faith?" Matt. 6:30

> "*Love not the world* [outward attention, loyalty to any organization], *neither the things* [attachments] *of the world* [outward attention]. *If any man love the world* [organized religious groups], *the love of the Father* [Pure consciousness of the ultimate Self] *is not in him.*" John 2:15

The verses clearly say that no one can serve two bosses at one time: namely, on the one hand, the righteous way of Guru-*parampara*, or being inward to reach the Source of mind, and, on the other hand, being involved in an organization and making oneself outward depending on supporting oneself through the polluted conditional donations rendered to an organization (which is a monster, or a beast, who demands loyalty, or otherwise threatens to put the dissenter's name on a black list or crush him).

> "... that the image of the beast [organization, or institution] *should both speak* [effectively], *and cause* [enforce] that as many as would not worship [be loyal to] the image of the beast [organization] should be killed [put in trouble]." Rev. 13:15

> "*And he* [the monster organization] *causeth all, both small and great, rich and poor, free and bond, to receive a mark* [loyalty to the organization, or attachment to religious groups] *in their right hand, or in their foreheads.*" Rev. 13:16

Someone may pose the question to the author, "Well, Mr. Author, from your limited personal experience, how can you make generalizations about the entire world?"

The author would humbly request the honorable reader to look to the pages of history from past to present where they will find that all the religious groups, due to their sectarian views and fanaticism, were, and are, fighting among themselves in the name of religion.

They simply do not even understand what the word religion means. They fight, and they disturb the harmony, rhythm and equilibrium state of blissful Consciousness, which is absolutely One.

> *"There is neither Jew nor Greek, there is neither bond nor free, there is neither male nor female. For ye are all one ... "* Gal. 3:28

The Sanskrit word for religion is *Dharma*, derived from the root verb *Dhri*, which means "that which holds." The Breath, or the *Prana*, holds life, so to achieve eternal Tranquility through the still state of Breath, or *Prana*, is *Dharma*, or religion.

> *"The Veda, Smriti, Sadachara, that is, Kriya, and the dear action of the self, that is, being tranquil [being one with the tranquil state of Consciousness] is the true religion."* Commentary on Manusanghita by Lahiri Mahasay, 2:12, p. 45

Spiritual organizations are a kind of "entertainment industry" for the so-called spiritual leaders of these organizations, where the emotional and devotional seekers of Truth, especially those who are spiritual novices, are exploited.

If the matter is adjudged with open mind and without any prejudice, then we will find the rarely-found righteous way — at least the righteous perspective.

Let us be honest and frank, and let us be righteous. The important and fundamental question here is which perspective one has. For example, if one says "guerrilla warfare" or "terrorist," from the perspective of one on the other side, the same thing will be adjudged or viewed as "freedom fighting" or "patriotism." It all matters which side of the fence one is on.

Babaji (the divine Himalayan Yogi, who is formally a Swami as well as being established in Antar *Sanyas*, that is, "internally detached") himself has not started organizations, neither does he support this.

Babaji's disciple, Lahiri Mahasay (the polestar of Kriya *Yoga* and great householder who is established in Antar *Sanyas*), repeatedly refused to allow his disciples to start organizations around the teachings of Kriya.

This is the true spirit of righteousness upheld by all the great Masters, realized Sages and Scriptures.

From the true spirit, or righteous perspective, receiving donations in the name of non-profit organizations and sustaining a better lifestyle in the name of spiritual progression is definitely not generating the quality of *Asteya* (non-stealing). The non-profit organization is not an "interest free" organization in the spiritual perspective, as donor and donee mutually profit.

From the other side's perspective, "non-profit" is balanced. It is noble. Receiving donations and serving others may be argued intellectually to be a noble activity, but from the strictly spiritual point of view, as well as from the point of view of righteousness, both the donor and donee are tricked by negative subtle forces to profit out of transactions individually.

Hence the whole consideration, from the perspective of inner realization, is a subtle trick, but this is not perceived by hermits living in the hermitages due to their attachments and confusion. To make progression in spiritual life, an honest way of living is very necessary.

Thus, following the Vedic tradition of having a natural household lifestyle, maintained by honest earnings, facilitates the seeker's good health, pure Breath, good sentiment and righteous energy, which help in contemplative life, or in Kriya practice, to achieve the tranquil state of Breath and, ultimately, the After-effect-poise of Kriya, that is, eternal Tranquility.

The subsistence from the organizations supported by accrued conditional donations pollutes the food, breath, sentiments and energy and puts the hermits into a confused state.

Fortunately, or unfortunately, this is the divine scheme, and there is no sense in arguing intellectually.

Some rules have exceptions. For example, the first (Adi) Sankaracharya, disciple of Babaji, (in the eighth century) founded four hermitages on all four sides of India and appointed his disciples to head these four hermitages (in a post called "Sankaracharya"), while he himself remained outside of post and position.

Understanding Kundalini

Kundalini means "coiled serpent" in Sanskrit. In yoga a "corporeal energy", an unconscious, instinctive or libidinal force or Shakti, lies coiled at the base of the spine. It is envisioned either as a goddess or else as a sleeping serpent. The **kundalini** resides in the sacrum bone in three and a half coils and has been described as a residual power of pure desire.

Not all **kundalini** experiences are identical and may vary in intensity and duration. Typically we meditate to arouse the **kundalini** and then to raise it through the body. You should remember that not all types of meditation or **yoga** are devoted to the awakening of **kundalini**. You may feel the sensation of heat at the base of the spine which could be warm or hot. The energy travels up a psychic pathway parallel to the spinal column. We have mentioned the **sushumna** earlier on in this writing. The **sushumna** is the central axis and is crisscrossed in a helix by the **ida** [ēd*o (Sanskrit) "comfort"] and **pingala** [pinggul*o (Sanskrit) "reddish"]. As it rises the **kundalini** activates the **chakra**s in succession. As the **kundalini** is rising the body may become cold and corpse-like as the **kundalini** leaves the lower portions and begins to rise. The meditator (yogi) may begin to shudder, tremble, or rock violently, feel extreme heat and cold, hear strange but pleasant sounds, and see various kinds of lights including an inner light. The objective is to raise the **kundalini** to the crown **chakra**, where it unites with the Shiva, or the male polarity, and brings illumination. It is then important to lower the energy to another chakra, but not below the heart **chakra**. By repeatedly raising the **kundalini** to the crown, the yogi will succeed in having the energy permanently stay there.

Some schools of thought on the **kundalini** energy is that the energy can be awakened by a **guru** (teacher), but the body and spirit must be prepared by such practices as **pranayama** and/or physical exercises, visualization, chanting. The **kundalini** can also awaken spontaneously.

Kundalini can also be awakened by the grace of a Siddha-**Guru** through shaktipat, or blessing. A Siddha **Guru** is a spiritual teacher, a master, whose identification with the supreme self is uninterrupted.

When **kundalini** rises to the head it unites itself with the Supreme Being and then the yogi becomes engrossed in deep meditation and infinite bliss. The arousing of **kundalini** is believed by some to be the only way of attaining Divine Wisdom. Self-Realization is the equivalent to Divine Wisdom and is the same as self-knowledge. The awakening of the **kundalini** shows itself as the awakening of inner knowledge and brings with it pure joy, pure knowledge and pure love.

In the 1950s scientists began to study altered states of consciousness in the laboratory. Later in the 1960s and 1970s many other studies were made. There is a whole range of phenomena in the process of the transformation that are constant and universal and go well beyond personal and cultural differences.

Some of the most common symptoms of **kundalini** awakening as listed by Wikipedia are:

- Involuntary jerks, tremors, shaking, itching, tingling, and crawling sensations, especially in the arms and legs
- Energy rushes or feelings of electricity circulating the body
- Intense heat (sweating) or cold, especially as energy is experienced passing through the **chakra**s
- Spontaneous **pranayama**, **asana**s, **mudra**s and **bandha**s
- Visions or sounds at times associated with a particular chakra
- Diminished sexual desire or a state of constant orgasm
- Emotional purgings in which particular emotions become dominant for short periods of time.

- Depression
- Pressure inside the skull and headache
- Bliss, feelings of infinite love and universal connectedness, transcendent awareness

There are many other symptoms which may be noticed and recognized. There is a need to know these symptoms as there may be many of these symptoms occurring for which you are unaware of what is really happening. Other notable symptoms could be:

Spontaneous body movements which can include any part of the body, including the eyes. These body movements may be smooth and sinuous, spasmodic and jerky, or vibratory. They can range from muscle twitching to prolonged trembling to the automatic assumption of difficult yogic postures known as **asana**s and **mudra**s. A person may assume these postures without prior knowledge of the yogic practices.

Unusual breathing patterns, **pranayama** or retention of breath, breath control. This can be evidenced as rapid breathing, shallow breathing, deep breathing, or extended breath retention.

Paralysis can occur during deep meditation whereby the body sometimes becomes temporarily locked into certain postures.

Tickling sensations whereby the skin or the inside of the body may tingle, tickle, itch, or vibrate. Sometimes this is felt as a deep ecstatic tickle and orgasmic feeling. These sensations can often start in the legs and feet or the pelvis and move up the back to the crown and then down over the forehead, the face, the throat, and to the abdomen.

Hot and cold sensations affecting either the whole body or parts of the body can also occur during the **kundalini** process

Seeing inner lights and visions may also occur during the awakening process. This vision has been described by various Swamis and Masters as visions of red light of the size of the whole body, or white or black spots, and of the lentil-sized "blue-pearl" in which the matrix of the universe can be seen. Sometimes the lights can be seen to illuminate specific areas of the body.. There have been experiences reported of inner light which is accompanied by the ability to see a darkened room as illuminated. Others have reported being able to perceive an aura or halo of light around the illumined mystic or enlightened being.

Inner sounds which are internally perceived include a variety of noises such as whistling, hissing, chirping, roaring, and flutelike or bell like sounds. The mystical sound known as the sacred syllable "**OM**" can also be heard internally.

Pain is an obvious sensation and can be reported in the head, the eyes, the spine, or other parts of the body. Sometimes the pain begins abruptly without any apparent cause and then vanishes just as abruptly and mysteriously as it began. This can last from several seconds to hours or sometimes days. Headaches are a common pain that may be felt during the **kundalini** awakening process. Itzhak Bentov addressed the issue of headaches in an interview with "New Age" magazine in March 1978. Mineda McCleave in 1978 wrote an article on this aspect and made these observations:

> "Tension headaches may be unrecognized symptoms of **kundalini** awakening. Migraine may be a precursor to **kundalini** activity, or an associated ailment. Cluster headaches, a form of particularly harsh headache that generally strikes males, might be explained by the cyclic nature of **kundalini**. These headaches tend to strike most often in the spring and the fall and though many theories are put forth, no one knows with any certainty why they are seasonal. Such headaches may last for half an hour to two hours, approximately, and then disappear for a short while, only to return several times daily, with pain severe enough to cause the victim to pace the floor in agony. They may occur in such clusters for weeks or months, and then completely disappear until the next cluster season."

Unusual or extreme emotion such as feelings of ecstasy, bliss, peace, love, devotion, joy, and cosmic harmony may occur just as readily as feelings of intense fear, anxiety, confusion, depression, and sometimes even hatred. In the later stages of the awakening process the feelings of bliss, peace, love, and contentment tend to predominate.

Distortions of thought processes which may include speeded up thinking, or slowed down thinking may occur.

Many other strange occurrences and paranormal phenomenon may also be present during this time.

These are not to be taken lightly. There are more symptoms than these and we shall look at some of the other symptoms which occur. Some of the more subtle symptoms which we look at can be present for short periods of time or can be present for many years. The awakening process as mentioned previously can be spontaneous or it can take several years to develop completely. Sometimes the symptoms have even been mistaken as mental illness.

The signs and symptoms usually described, such as shifts in emoting and thinking as well as seeing of visions and the hearing of voices seem to be largely determined by personal factors. However the physical sensations such as itching, fluttering, tingling, intense heat and cold, perceptions of inner lights, and perceptions of primary sounds, spasms and contortions seem to be features of certain phases of the process.

In understanding the process of the **kundalini** awakening it is necessary to discuss the various aspects of the seven **chakras**. The **chakra**s or wheels are vortices present in the body and are known as the centers or seats of power. They are commonly depicted as lotus flowers with varying numbers of petals which correspond to different forms of energy which is associated with each center.

The root **chakra** is associated with the earth element, the sense of smell, the feet and the general distribution of the life-force or **prana** in the body.

The next **chakra** in ascending order is located in the genital area. It is associated with the sense of taste, the hands and sexuality. This **chakra** is known as the sacral **chakra**.

Next we have the third **chakra**, which is the solar plexus, located in the region of the navel. Some traditions believe that his **chakra** is an alternative resting place for the dormant **kundalini**. It is connected with the fire element, digestion, the anus, and the sense of light. Hence you remember one of the important steps we learned in the ancient technique of meditation was the pressing of the heel upon the **perineum** to activate and help awaken the **kundalini**.

The fourth center is the heart **chakra**. It is the location for the eternal sound of "**OM**". The heart **chakra** is associated with the air element, the sense of touch, feelings, the genitals and the stimulation of **prana**.

The fifth **chakra** is the throat **chakra** connected with the ether element, the sense of hearing, the mouth and the skin.

The sixth **chakra** is located on the forehead between the brows and is known as the command center or the Third Eye. It is associated with the mind and is the center where the teacher can contact the disciple telepathically.

The seventh **chakra** or crown **chakra** is the thousand petal lotus or thousand spokes or the energy pathways of the center. It is located at the crown of the head where the soft spot of newborn babies is located. It is responsible for the experience of overwhelming light and bliss that are the results when the **kundalini** rises from the lowest center to the crown center. As explained by Gopi Krishna:

"Whenever I turned my mental eye upon myself I invariably perceived a luminous glow within and outside my head in a state of constant vibration, as if a jet of an extremely subtle and brilliant substance rising through the spine spread itself out of the cranium, filling and surrounding it with an indescribable radiance."

In addition to the **chakra**s another important part of the process of **kundalini** awakening is the three major pathways along which the **kundalini** energy travels. These pathways are known as the **nadi**s. The symbol on the right, the caduceus, commonly represents medicine. The center pathway is known as the **sushumna** and connects all of the seven **chakra**s. The other two wrap around the **sushumna** in helix fashion. The channel to the left is known as the **ida** and the channel to the right is known as the **pingala**. The two helical channels pass each other at the various centers until they merge in the sixth **chakra**, the Third Eye.

The right channel has a heating function and the left channel is the cooling function. It is very important that in order to avoid unpleasant or even dangerous side effects that the awakened **kundalini** must be guided through the central channel alone. As the **kundalini** awakens and travels upwards it passes through the various **chakra**s and clears and awakens those **chakra**s or centers and those centers then become active. The **kundalini** temporarily energizes the chakra and then absorbs its energy. By the time the **kundalini** reaches the top center the rest of the body is depleted of bioenergy and hence the lower extremities tend to become cold and corpselike.

As the **kundalini** moves into the Third Eye and crown then the intense experience of bliss and light are experienced. This experience is a formless ecstasy which is known as nirvikalpa **samadhi**.

In the beginning, the first full ascent of the **kundalini** energy may lasts for only a brief time, maybe only seconds or minutes. Then the **kundalini** moves back down into one of the lower **chakra**s. It is important to repeat the process as often as possible until the **kundalini** resides permanently in the crown **chakra**. It is also important that when allowing the **kundalini** to return to a lower chakra that you consciously guide it to return no lower than the heart **chakra**. When the **kundalini** returns to the lower three chakras there is generally some dangers of this including ego inflation and maybe even rampant sexual desires. Other problems may also become apparent if the awakened **kundalini** is allowed to return to the lower three **chakra**s.

As the **kundalini** awakening process occurs it is moving in an upward motion towards the 2 uppermost **chakra**s. During this process it will encounter various obstacles or knots. These obstacles can be present causing blockages anywhere along the path and can be looked upon as stress points. It is important to pierce through each obstacle by way of single-minded concentration through the meditation process and focused breath. As the **kundalini** moves upwards and encounters these blockages there may be some pain involved as it works its way through the stress point until the blockage is dissolved. Once that blockage is removed the **kundalini** proceeds freely through that point and continues on its upward path until it meets the next blockage. And then the process of removing and working through this stress point is repeated. It is possible that the **kundalini** can be working at removing several blockages simultaneously.

Gopi Krishna had psychic experiences as a child but later became an agnostic as a young man. He meditated regularly for many years and had no mystical experiences of any kind until about 17 years after he began to meditate on a regular basis. At that time he experienced a spontaneous arousal of the kundalini that radically changed his life. Then some 6 years later he had a powerful **kundalini** experience leading to **samadhi**. He wrote of that experience:

> " I distinctly felt an incomparably blissful sensation in all my nerves moving from the tips of fingers and toes and other parts of the trunk and limbs towards the spine, where, concentrated and intensified, it mounted upwards with a still more exquisitely pleasant feeling to pour into the upper region of the brain a rapturous and exhilarating stream of a rare radiating nerve secretion. In the absence of a more suitable appellation, I call it nectar."[9]

This blissful sensation vanished when he paid attention to if, but it would flow upward with growing intensity so long as he ignored it. He goes on to explain that suddenly, like a roar of a waterfall he felt a stream of liquid light entering his brain through the spinal cord. His body began to rock and he was enclosed in a halo of light. He became one with his surroundings and was overwhelmed with bliss.

This was followed by feelings of terror, weakness, and indifference to people. His mouth tasted bitter, his throat felt scorched and frequently his whole body felt as if it was pierced by countless hot pins. He suffered from insomnia. He noted that in the dark he could see a reddish glow around himself. Once the **kundalini** process had been awakened Gopi Krishna reported that he was completely at its mercy. It took many years for him to attain a state of physical balance. But once the **kundalini** was

---

[9] Krishna, Gopi 1971. *Kundalini: Evolutionary Energy in Man*. Berkeley: Shambala, p. 186.

stabilized it formed the basis for the gradual development of extraordinary mental gifts, creativity, and tranquility. It led to all kinds of mystical experiences as well.

I would also like to point out that the **kundalini** awakening process can start in your youth, then go dormant. It may then reappear later in life. Or it may reappear later when you decide to take up a routine of meditation. The awakening can be spontaneous or can take longer periods of time to make its way up the spine through the blockages, sometimes taking years to complete the process. So that it may be that you have some of the symptoms listed above early in life then no more occurrences and then suddenly upon taking up meditation the occurrences may start up again or take on another form.

Since many of these are very often unexplainable from a medical point of view it is wise for the yogi to be aware of some of the symptoms that have been reported over the ages by those who have been through the kundalini awakening process. This does not necessarily mean that you will experience all of the symptoms. It also does not mean that you will experience any of the uncomfortable symptoms. As noted previously it could very well be determined on what you came to this incarnation with in terms of your past life experiences with regards to inner awakening and mystical experiences. There are any number of factors which can determine the outcome of the individual person's experience although the final outcome of the awakening is generally the same, i.e. self-realization, cosmic consciousness, **samadhi**.

Therefore as you proceed with more advanced techniques in the process of meditation it is necessary that you learn to self-pace your development. This includes the **kriya yoga** techniques which are practiced during the meditation. If ill-effects are evident then it is advisable to lessen the amount of **kriya**s being performed and then to gradually increase them at a later date.

Kriya yoga is a powerful technique which in conjunction with the other techniques will lead to kundalini awakening. Many organizations will make their disciples take an oath to do only a certain number of **Kriya**s per day and then to receive permission to accelerate the amount of **Kriya**s allowed in a meditation sitting. However I believe that each person knows their own limits better than any organization knows them and therefore each individual person can better pace themselves for their own development.

This is also true because of the fact that time has speeded up as noted in the acceleration of time in the chapter listed on the Mayan Calendar. If individuals are going to be prepared for the "shift" then it is important that each person take responsibility for his own development at a pace which that person is comfortable with. Some people may go faster or slower than others. This is perfectly all right.

I also think that this is a good time to remind you that if you have not taken steps to revive the **pineal** gland then you should do so now by adding iodine to your diet. No amount of meditation or **kriya**s is going to help you toward **kundalini** awakening if the **pineal** gland is in a calcified state. Please refer to the chapter on "The Importance of the Pineal Gland" if you need to refresh your memory on this important aspect of your routine.

The Great Love Story

Om Namah Shivaya [Ōm Num*o Shēv*oyu], "I bow to Shiva [Shēvu]". This is a very powerful **mantra** and it is said that this **mantra** vibrates continually in the heart. All mantras are traditionally done for 108 times twice a day for a period of at least 40 days. You will need a traditional set of **Mala** beads for this. **Mala** beads typically come in a length of 108 beads with 1 extra bead, the turning bead, to mark the end of the counting rotation. **Mala** beads are used for the counting of sacred mantras and chants. They come in a variety of materials. However, the most widely accepted by yogis is the sandalwood, as it is considered to be divine and have a scent which is cherished by the deities.

So now you are probably wondering what this has to do with the great love story and what is this great love story? It is a love story that is a part of each one of our lives and is with us through each of our incarnations. It is a love we are continually seeking.

There are many stories about Lord Shiva and Shakti, his wife. This one is paraphrased and explains how it encompasses our experiences.

In this story we have the characters Lord Shiva and Goddess Shakti. We also have the **kundalini** which is associated with creation and viewed as a thin silver thread.

Lord Shiva resides in our crown **chakra** sitting upon his lotus-flower throne. Shakti resides as a coil of **kundalini** at our root **chakra**, usually depicted as a coiled snake.

Shiva sits on his throne deep in his own thoughts and is oblivious to anything going on in the lower **chakra**s, including Shakti's root **chakra**. Shiva is on his lotus-flower throne, in his cave, performing many meditations and producing much heat and energy, and developing much knowledge, but it goes nowhere because this heat, energy and knowledge of Shiva must be united with the **kundalini** of Shakti in order to be of any real purpose.

Everyday Shakti tries to raise the **kundalini** and entice Shiva to come out of his cave. She sends beautiful thoughts to Shiva, adorns him with flowers and blessings, and pays him great homage, but to no avail.

Shakti continues to raise the **kundalini** to entice Shiva, and adorn him with flowers. The power of Shakti's devotion and persistence of meditation finally shakes Shiva out of his meditations and he opens his Third Eye and comes out of his cave and accepts Shakti as his wife.

Therefore we must continually be persistent to shake Lord Shiva off his throne and have him meet Shakti on her journey of the **kundalini** up and down the spinal column. Once this meeting takes place, it is the opening of the upper chakras, mainly the Third Eye and then the crown, and is what is commonly known as enlightenment.

What happens when Shiva and Shakti meet? This is known as the **kundalini** experience and is the awakening of the crown chakra. The crown **chakra** is known as the thousand-petal lotus and is located at the crown of the head and is representative of the experience of overwhelming light and bliss that is the result when the **kundalini** force rises from the lowest center (the root chakra) to the crown center. It is white and sheds a constant and profuse stream of nectar and light.

Light is an important aspect of the **kundalini** awakening. There is also another very important aspect of this process, which should not be avoided. When the energy rises up and down the spinal column there are actually three major pathways involved. The center of the spine which is known as the **sushumna** is what we have been working with. The other two pathways (**nadis**) are the **ida** and the **pingala** and these two **nadis** wrap around the

sushumna passing each other in helix fashion at the various chakras on the way up the spinal column to the crown chakra.

The left pathway is known as the **ida nadi** starts at the left and is a cooling function for the body. The right pathway is the **pingala nadi** and starts at the right and is a heating function for the body. It is most important to guide the **kundalini** energy only through the center column. To use the other two pathways will lead to uncomfortable and even dangerous side effects.

So now we will place our **mantra** to Lord Shiva in our meditation practice. *Om Namah Shivaya* is our silent inward chant that we will use. This **mantra** is done twice daily for at least 40 days. You can do it longer if you desire, but not less than 40 days. The **mantra** is always performed while focusing on the Third Eye and visualizing Lord Shiva sitting on the lotus-flower throne. It is also always performed while using the rhythm of the rocking boat *(***navi kriya***)*.

ROUTINE:
Pranayama (20-minute session)
Chin churn (**jalandhara mudra**)
Abdominal Pump
With **Hong-Sau** (**Hong** on inhalation and **Sau** on exhalation)
With **kriya** breathing technique
With tongue pressed upward and back (**kechari mudra**)
With the mouth closed and silently chanting
With flexing of the anal sphincter (**mulabandha***)*
With focusing on the Third Eye (**shambhavi mudra***)*
With the rhythm of the rocking boat (**navi kriya**)
Then do **yoni mudra**
Deep Meditation (70-minute session)
3 cycles of **navi kriya OM** counts
Then follow with the **mantra** *Om Namah Shivaya [Ōm Num*o Shēv*oyu]* 108 counts
Focus on Third Eye
Visualize in third-eye Lord Shiva on the lotus-flower throne
Use the rocking boat rhythm of the **navi kriya**

Use **kriya** breathing
Keep mouth closed and silently chanting
Then follow with the **sutra**s
Then follow with deep meditation of **OM**
    Keep the energy rising and falling
    Focus on the Third Eye
    Use **kriya** breathing
    Inwardly chant **OM** on the inhalation and **OM** on the exhalation.
    Move towards the stillness inside.
    Meditate upon the nothingness and silence within

Revelation

After about an hour of meditation techniques, the meditator may be energized to the point of **samadhi**. **Samadhi** is merging the little self with the big Self. How is this done?

A yogi knows that all is one. The illusion of multiplicity is because of veils, or barriers. The veils separate A from Not A. This is duality—hot/cold, left/right, high/low, etc. In general, positive/negative. What happens when the veils are lifted? One could reason that there would be neutrality or zero. But the realm of unity (7th level) is beyond reason (3rd level). Imagine that The One (God) is the central star, radiating light. Imagine the veils are curtains, casting shadows. The shadows would be the negative to the sun's positive. So removing the veils ("revealing") leaves just sunlight—an infinity of positiveness. So the yogi moves from limitation and duality of positive and negative to infinity and unity of positive. The One, God, is love, bliss, health, strength, and wisdom, without any hatred, sorrow, illness, weakness or foolishness. That is not logical, but God is beyond logic.

As the crown chakra opens from the movement of the *kundalini* energy the lower extremities will become cold and corpselike. The upper most part of the body will be filled with light and the intense experience of bliss, light, and superlucidity. At first this experience may last for only a few minutes and be very brief. But as time goes on the **kundalini** force will lengthen until it resides permanently in the crown center.

Experientially, motionlessness, silence and darkness of the senses gives way to weightless and floating in space; not exactly outer space, but more inner space. The yogi barely perceives the body. Instead there is a purple or violet cloud of energy, or more exactly energy/matter/time/space. Joy and wonder stirs and swirls. It's an all-consuming experience, like being in the womb, or a thrill that a child can have. The yogi wonders—Do I deserve this? Am I worthy of being in the presence of God? Can I be good enough to merge with God? The yogi eventually replies—I am a child of God; God forgives my trespasses if I forgive my trespasses. Yes, yes I am the prodigal son who has come home into the open arms of my Father. Yes! Ahhhh!

****

Samadhi is union with the universe, that is, achieving Christ, Krishna or cosmic consciousness.

A soul is a piece of divine consciousness. Divine consciousness is infinite. What is a piece of infinity? Infinity! $\infty/1,000,000,000 = \infty$. Or add as many zeros as you want, the result is still infinity. But the embodied soul is so identified with the limited body that it becomes accustomed to finitude.

Yet look at what the Bible says: "God created man in his own image" (Genesis 1:27). Because God is infinite, His image must also be infinite. A perfect image is holographic, that is, contains everything that is in the original image, though it may be smaller. This explains Jesus's statement "In my Father's house are many mansions" (John 14:2). This seemingly illogical statement makes sense when one considers that a small holographic piece of the universe contains the whole universe. Jesus was talking about holograms!

So where does this leave us? Follow this reasoning to its logical conclusion. Each of us is a soul, not a body. This soul is made in the image of God. Therefore it is infinite. It contains the whole universe. Strip away any thought of bodily limitations. The soul is energy, not heavy matter. Energy is forever flowing. Feel the energy that is flowing around your essence. Gravity has no effect on the ball of energy that is you. You are floating, even flying. Without thought of the body, you have no limits. Whatever is in your consciousness is a hologram of the universe. You are actually one with the universe! "The kingdom of God is within you" (Luke 17:21) Feel the thrill of that realization! Because love is merging,

merging with infinity leads to infinite love. And being in the center of infinite energy means there is only light. Shadows are a lack of light, and so are negative. But in brilliant light there is only positive—peace, abundance, and especially bliss. Do you feel infinite love and bliss as you embrace all of creation? It's wonderful how logic can lead to **samadhi**, if you only let it!

Samadhi does not come all at once for the new yogi, but comes in stages. Typically there are 4 beginning stages of **samadhi**. The Yogi will learn to recognize these stages as entrancing occurs, and in the end will move toward the final stages of **samadhi** with just a momentary passing of the first few stages.

The first stage of **samadhi** that is experienced by the yogi is a feeling of bliss and joy, a feeling of joyful peace within oneself. As this stage passes the yogi moves into the second phase of **samadhi** which is the presence of the bliss and joyfulness, but also the mind becomes more peaceful, and tranquillity of the mind becomes more pronounced. The yogi may notice a buzzing in the ears and around the upper portion of the body, and is drawn into the experience. A throbbing or pulsating feeling at the 3rd eye may also be felt at this time.

As the yogi enters the third stage of **samadhi**, a deeper level of tranquility and equanimity of the mind takes place. The sounds in the room are present, but appear to be just passing through the body—a non-dual experience. The yogi may be aware of the sounds, but the sounds have no impact upon the yogi; there is no identity of sensation. The yogi is a being, an empty conduit. Cosmic phenomena begin to arise at this stage. Sounds of the chakras are heard. Visions may be present.

The next stage of **samadhi** is the feeling of being so relaxed that the yogi feels as he could meditate forever. This stage will usually occur after 1 or more hours of sitting in meditation. The yogi can become breathless, or at least not having any awareness of the breathing process. A total at-one-ness occurs and the meditation could go on for many hours or even days, if so desired.

At this point of the crown opening and the *kundalini* experience it is important that the energy be redirected during meditation. When following the energy flow of the kundalini it is now important to keep the energy flowing between the crown and the heart chakra (not below the heart chakra).

The Excellence of Kriya Yoga

When a person performs **kriya yoga** there are some mathematical consequences that are accomplished as a result of the breathing technique involved. When one first learns **kriya** the breathing technique is not as listed below. However these calculations will give you an idea on what to work towards. It is not a matter of holding one's breath for the allotted time, but it is a matter of practice, and as one practices then the breath is naturally lengthened to be near or at what is listed in the calculations. Lahiri Mahasay worked out the math as follows:

1. 12 excellent **kriya**s result in withdrawal from the senses.
2. 144 excellent **kriya**s result in realization or soul-oriented visualization.
3. 1728 excellent **kriya**s result in being fixed in soul-visualization.
4. 20,736 excellent **kriya**s result in **samadhi**.

Lahiri Mahasay also states that just as food causes appeasement of hunger, similarly **kriya yoga** causes attainment of God.

He elaborated further saying that an ordinary person inhales and exhales 21,600 times in a 24-hour period of time. Everyone inhales and exhales 15 times per minute. When there is a depletion of the resources of breath, a living being expires. But the time taken for one **kriya** is 44 seconds. By this calculation a yogi practices 1964 (about 2000) **kriya**s in 24 hours, meaning a yogi inhales and exhales 2000 times in a day whereas an ordinary person inhales and exhales 21,600 times. By practicing continual **kriya** Yoga, a yogi will eventually achieve the static state when breathing becomes motionless, commonly known as breathless **samadhi**.

If you have received instruction from me in **kriya** Yoga then you have received the instruction as it was taught by Lahiri Mahasay. You are probably now wondering what is an "excellent" **kriya**. An excellent **kriya** as noted in the above mathematical presentations by Lahiri Mahasay refers to **Kechari mudra**.

Kechari mudra is often referred to as swallowing the tongue. **Kechari mudra** is the entry of the tongue backward and upward into the palatal cavity during meditation. It is known as stage 6 of **kriya yoga**, and is proclaimed to be the ultimate in spiritual attainment, overcoming disease and death.

Kechari mudra is achieved in stages. We have already covered stage 1, which raises the tongue to the top of the mouth while meditating. The tongue is held at the point where the hard and soft palates meet at the top of the mouth.

Stage 2 is pushing back further to the end of the soft palate and reaching behind the uvula and pushing upwards to the edge of the nasal spectrum.

Stage 3 is entering the palatal cavity, the nasal pharynx.

Stage 4 is pushing further upwards within the palatal cavity to the top. It will be necessary to turn the tongue towards the center and push upward on its side.

Upon trying **kechari mudra** you will most likely find that your tongue is too short. You need to stretch the tongue and release the restriction (frenum) below the tongue. The best stretching exercise is to grab the tongue with a dry piece of fabric and pull the tongue outwards, paying close attention to pulling it in all directions, from side to side and downwards. Hold the tongue in the outstretched position with the fabric, thereby stretching the tongue. This can be repeated several times throughout the day.

Kechari mudra is the most sought after and desired outcome of yogic practices. It is well worth the effort. It may take several years to achieve. It is only achieved by those who have great devotion to pursue this highest attainment.

However, even with all the above, it is a very difficult task to achieve. Later we will learn another method which will give the effects of **kechari mudra** without having to achieve the "swallowing the tongue" method.

UFOs and Flying Saucers?

(**Merkaba** [murkubu (Egyptian) "light-spirit-body"], also spelled **merkabah**, is the divine light vehicle used by ascended masters to connect with and reach those in tune with the higher realms. "Mer" means Light. "Ka" means Spirit. "Ba" means Body. Mer-Ka-Ba means the spirit/body surrounded by counter-rotating fields  of light, (wheels within wheels), spirals of energy as in DNA, which transports the spirit/body from one dimension to another.

In modern esoteric teachings, it is taught that the **merkaba** is an interdimensional vehicle consisting of two equally sized, interlocked tetrahedra of light with a common center, where one tetrahedron points up and the other down. This point symmetric form is called a stella octangula or stellated octahedron which can also be obtained by extending the faces of a regular octahedron until they intersect again.

In his books, researcher and physicist Drunvalo Melchizedek describes this figure as a "Star Tetrahedron", since it can be viewed as a three dimensional Star of David. By imagining two superimposed "star tetrahedrons" as counterrotating, along with specific **prana** breathing techniques, certain eye movements and **mudra**s, it is taught that one can activate a non-visible saucer-shaped energy field around the human body that is anchored at the base of the spine.

The varieties of benefits of using the **merkaba** are greatly varied: It is a most powerful healing and protection tool. By utilizing the ancient **prana** breathing technique, we are able to restore the **prana** flow through the **pineal** gland at the center of our brain. This revived use of our gland, which has been virtually dormant for 13,000 years, allows the heightened use of our telepathic and extrasensory perception abilities.

The **merkaba** balances and revives the activities between the two sides of our brain. Such training strengthens our sensitivities and mental abilities. The **merkaba** assists us in our spiritual growth. It connects us with our higher self, i.e. ourself on a higher level of consciousness.

The **merkaba** enables us to feel unconditional love, thus healing ourselves as well as others. It gives us the possibility of creating any kind of harmonious reality we desire. The **merkaba** can be "programmed" to do anything, the only limitation being our own beliefs and imagination.

The **merkaba** is also a tool that can be used to transcend into other dimensions and can also be used as the ascension meditation. Revived studies and practices of the **merkaba** are emerging all over the world after many years of being suppressed from different sources, including the Old Testament and Kabala.

Although Drunvalo teaches that the **merkaba** was used in the ancient mystery schools of Egypt it is also the most ancient teaching of the Kabala, the occult and mystical tradition within Judaism. There are references to the **merkaba** meditation being practiced as far back as the second century B.C.

According to Manly Hall in *The Secret Teachings Of All Ages*:

Ceremonial magic is the ancient art of invoking and controlling spirits by a scientific application of certain formulæ. A magician, enveloped in sanctified vestments and carrying a wand inscribed with hieroglyphic figures, could by the power vested in certain words and symbols control the invisible inhabitants of the elements and of the astral world. While the elaborate ceremonial magic of antiquity was not necessarily evil, there arose from its perversion several false schools of sorcery, or *black magic*.

Egypt, a great center of learning and the birthplace of many arts and sciences, furnished an ideal environment for transcendental experimentation. Here the black magicians of Atlantis continued to exercise their superhuman powers until they had completely undermined and corrupted the morals of the primitive Mysteries. By establishing a sacerdotal caste they usurped the position formerly occupied by the initiates, and seized the reins of spiritual government. Thus black magic dictated the state religion and paralyzed the intellectual and spiritual activities of the individual by demanding his complete and unhesitating acquiescence in the dogma formulated by the priestcraft. The Pharaoh became a puppet in the hands of the Scarlet Council — a committee of arch-sorcerers elevated to power by the priesthood.

These sorcerers then began the systematic destruction of all keys to the ancient wisdom, so that none might have access to the knowledge necessary to reach adeptship without first becoming one of their order. They mutilated the rituals of the Mysteries while professing to preserve them, so that even though the neophyte passed through the degrees he could not secure the knowledge to which he was entitled. Idolatry was introduced by encouraging the worship of the images which in the beginning the wise had erected solely as symbols for study and meditation. False interpretations were given to the emblems and figures of the Mysteries, and elaborate theologies were created to confuse the minds of their devotees. The masses, deprived of their birthright of understanding and groveling in ignorance, eventually became the abject slaves of the spiritual impostors. Superstition universally prevailed and the black magicians completely dominated national affairs, with the result that humanity still suffers from the sophistries of the priestcrafts of Atlantis and Egypt.

Fully convinced that their Scriptures sanctioned it, numerous medieval Qabbalists devoted their lives to the practice of ceremonial magic. The transcendentalism of the Qabbalists is founded upon the ancient and magical formula of King Solomon, who has long been considered by the Jews as the prince of ceremonial magicians.[10]

The **merkaba** was combined with meditation, prayer, and yogic postures in such a way that the practitioners ascended or descended in their **merkaba** to other realms or dimensions of reality.

So what is a **merkaba**? It is the divine light vehicle used by the Masters to connect with and reach those in tune with the higher realms. The **merkaba** is the vehicle of Light mentioned in the Bible by Ezekiel.

The **merkaba** meditation can be learned by two separate methods. One is the masculine method and the other is the feminine method. Since the masculine method is very mind-based and encompasses many steps to achieve. It is not a very quick way

---

[10] Hall, Manly P. 1928. *The Secret Teachings of All Ages*. Self-published.

of mastering the meditation. The meditation can be learned by the masculine method of the 17 breaths and memorized. However, it may take years of concentrated effort to achieve inter-dimensional experiences in this manner, whereas the feeling or feminine method can work in less than 2 breaths. Therefore the feminine way of achieving the **merkaba** will be taught within these writings.

STEP 10: Merkaba and Heart Center Meditation

So now that we have set ourselves upon a firm foundation of meditation from the ancient traditional methods of meditating we can put all of our efforts and skills into one meditation which will help us during the forthcoming periods of change which are about to become evident to the planet on which we live.

To summarize, we have learned several important foundational steps that will be used to successfully transport us within our **merkaba**s. If you have skipped any of those steps in the beginning, then it is time that you stop and go back and learn them. For without the strong foundation you will not be able to achieve this next step.

Be sure that you have also incorporated into your lifestyle the higher doses of iodine which is so needed to open the **pineal** gland to the experiences which will come.

Also it is important that you have been drinking your pink color charged water to fill your Heart Center with more love.

If you have incorporated these into your lifestyle then you are ready to move on into the higher steps.

To begin with, you will be sitting cross-legged with your heel tucked under and pressing against the **perineum**. Or if you are physically unable to sit in this position then you have your tennis ball or some other object that you are using to place in position instead of the heel of your foot.

As soon as you press against the **perineum** you should be able to feel the slight change in energy. Inhale a long **kriya yoga** breath, not so long that you are uncomfortable, bringing the prana energy down into the crown **chakra** and down the spine at the same time bringing the **prana** energy up from the root **chakra** and up the spine. The two points of energy will meet at the Heart Center.

The tongue during this process has been placed on the point between the soft and hard palate which further excites the energy moving in the spine. Just make the tongue a little thick and draw it backwards a little and place it over this portion of the upper mouth where the soft and hard palate meet. You should draw down a bit on this thick part of the tongue so that you feel as though you are sucking on something in your mouth.

The hand position is a choice of two, whichever is more relaxing for you. You may hold the hands with interlaced fingers comfortably in your lap with thumbs touching and pointing upwards or you may place the right hand palm up resting upon the left hand palm up with the thumbs touching and pointing upwards. Now on the exhale of the **kriya** yoga breath you will direct the flow of energy outwards from the Heart Center. At this point you will feel the energy flowing through your arms and surrounding your body and flowing outwards. You will also begin to feel the slight rotation of spiraling energy fields around you. This is the forming of the **merkaba**.

Continue to take **kriya yoga** breaths and direct the exhalations outward from the heart area. Continue to press the thick part of the tongue at the sensitive point between the soft and hard palates of the mouth. Relax as the **merkaba** begins to spin faster and faster. Even out your **kriya yoga** breathing so that it becomes more concentrated and shallow. Squeezing the epiglottis and constricting the air flow will direct the breath more into the nasal cavity and stimulate the upper portions of the cavity more acutely.

Feel the energies rising and falling within the spinal column, feel the lightheadedness of the spinning of the **merkaba** around you, feel the bliss coming on, and all of a sudden you are transported.

Where you go is between you and your higher self. Your spirit guides, ascended masters, and teachers will be there with you.

During this period of time it is possible to visit other realms, gain knowledge from the ascended Masters, experience the visions of the future and the past, **samadhi**, etc.

You may also want to add your **yoga sutras** into this meditation as they are much more powerful here. You learned the **yoga sutras** in Step 5 in a previous chapter. A more advanced way of doing the **sutras** is to integrate them here within the **merkaba** and the Heart Center meditation.

As the energy is being drawn up to the crown chakra you will remember that it is also necessary to bring the energy back down. So we bring the energy back down only to the heart **chakra** which has formed the **merkaba**. Now on the exhalation of the **kriya** yoga breath you will direct the flow of energy outwards from the Heart Center. At this point you will feel the energy flowing through your arms and surrounding your body and flowing outwards. As you exhale the **kriya** you repeat your first **sutra**. You continue this process through all of the **sutras**. It is not necessary to repeat them more than twice each as this is all that is needed to send them into the universe.

The **merkaba** meditation has been called the vehicle of ascension because it allows you to ascend and transcend the Earthly realm in which we inhabit.

Party Time

The coming **Pole Shift** is the biggest event on Earth since the Deluge, or Flood, which was caused by a close encounter with Nibiru, or Planet X. Nibiru, a large planet/brown dwarf star with a very elongated orbit, will come close to the Earth again in 2012. Magnetic and gravitational interactions add energy to the Earth, resulting in more tornados, hurricanes, volcanic eruptions and earthquakes. Most importantly, the boundary between the crust and mantle will liquify, allowing the entire crust to slip easily and quickly. It seems amazing that the Galactic Alignment (Earth, Sun and center of the Milky Way) occurs with a close approach of Nibiru (and the tightening economic and political death grip of the New World Order).

You've done the hard work, preparing for humanity's graduation, the **Pole Shift**. Ascended Masters and my spirit guide, Archangel Michael, have shared with me that, starting with the **Pole Shift**, inhabitants of Earth will acquire cosmic consciousness. Not full-blown cosmic consciousness of knowing everything and experiencing everything, but rather hearing each other's thoughts, and feeling connected to creation. Those who haven't dealt with their own range of thoughts will feel overwhelmed by the incessant thoughts of others, and will believe they are going stark-raving mad. But meditators will welcome the "free" **samadhi**, feeling love and bliss. This is the Cosmic Party. Everyone is invited to the Party, but only about ten percent will attend. It's strictly BYOB (Bring Your Own Bliss), because no one can give you bliss. The Photon Band will be playing. (That's a portion of light-filled space.) 2012 is party time!

Open Portal

Now that your obstacles have been removed and meditation techniques have been practiced, soar through the portal into the Spirit World.

Glossary

Pronunciation of Sanskrit and technical terms is indicated by NuEnglish, a spelling reform of English. Stress is on the first syllable, or after the asterisk (*). Vowels without the long mark (mācron) are short.

ajna ujnu (Sanskrit) "Third Eye"

akasha uk*oshu (Sanskrit) "inner space"

asana osunu (Sanskrit) "posture"

AUM See **OM**

bandha bundu (Sanskrit) "lock"

Bhagavad Gita Buguvud Gētu (Sanskrit) "Song of the Blessed One" A portion of the Mahabharata, having the form of a dialogue between the hero Arjuna and his charioteer, the avatar Krishna.

bhakti buktē (Sanskrit) "devotion; love of God"

bija bēju (Sanskrit) "seed"

chakra chukru (Sanskrit) "wheel, vortex" One of 7 major centers: Base, Sex, Solar Plexus, Heart, Throat, Third Eye and Crown. The **ida** and **pingala** channels cross at each chakra.

corpus callosum kōrpus kul*ōsum (Latin) "callused or firm body" The connection between the 2 hemispheres of the brain.

guru gurū (Sanskrit) " dispeller of darkness"

Hong-Sau Haung Sau (Sanskrit) "I am He"

ida ēd*o (Sanskrit) "comfort" One of the spinal channels.

ishta ishtu (Sanskrit) "an ideal"

jalandhara jolund*oru (Sanskrit) "chin"

karma kormu (Sanskrit) "deed; cause and effect"

kechari kāchur*ē (Sanskrit) "flying through inner space"

kevala kāvulu (Sanskrit) "absolute [knowledge]." Omni-science of a liberated soul.

kriya krēyu (Sanskrit) "technique" Techniques using **pranayama** to rapidly accelerate spiritual development.

kumbhaka kumb*uku (Sanskrit) "suspension of breath"

kundalini kundul*ēnē (Sanskrit) "coiled serpent"

mahasamadhi muh*o-sum*odē (Sanskrit) "great **samadhi**" The conscious final exit from the body.

mala [molu (Sanskrit) "garland"] Refers to a string of beads used to count **kriya**s.

mantra muntru (Sanskrit) "speech" A specially chosen syllable or series of syllables that is used in the practice of deep meditation.

medulla oblongata med*ulu oblaungg*otu (Latin) "long marrow" The lowest, hindmost part of the brain, continuous with the spinal cord.

Merkaba Murkubu (Egyptian) "light-spirit-body"

mudra mudr*o (Sanskrit) "spiritual gesture"   Various physical postures and maneuvers that direct ecstatic energy toward higher levels of manifestation in the nervous system.

mula mūlu (Sanskrit) "root"

nadi nodē (Sanskrit) "channel"   Nadis are the subtle (spiritual) nerves corresponding with the physical nerves.

nauli noulē (Sanskrit) "churn"

navi novē (Sanskrit) "navel; boat"

nidra nēdru (Sanskrit) "sleep"   A state of conscious deep sleep for extreme relaxation and subtler spiritual exploration.

nirvana nurv*onu (Sanskrit) "blowing out; extinction of the self"   The state of freedom from **karma**, and extinction of desire, passion, illusion and the self, and attainment of rest, truth and unchanging being; salvation.

OM ŌM, also **AUM** OŪM (Sanskrit) "**mantra** for the primordial vibration of God"

Patanjali Put*unjulē Sanskritic grammarian and compiler of the *Yoga Sutras*, a brief and enomorously influential work of 196 **sutra**s.

perineum perin* ēum (Latin and Greek) "around evacuation" The space between the genitals and anus.

pineal pīnēul (Latin) "of a pine [cone]"

pingala pinggul*o (Sanskrit) "reddish"   One of the spinal channels.

Pole Shift Not a change in direction of the Earth's axis, but a slippage of the entire Earth's crust on the mantle. More accurately, a "crustal shift."

prana pronu (Sanskrit) "breath" Also called life force, life energy, vital force and chi, or chee.

pranayama pronu-yomu (Sanskrit) "breath-control"

Rig Veda Rig Vādu (Sanskrit) "praise knowledge"

sahaja suh*oju (Sanskrit) "natural"

samadhi sum*odē (Sanskrit) "superconscious perception"

samyama sum-yomu (Sanskrit) "together control"

shambhavi shombuvē (Sanskrit) "furrowing of the brow" This is focusing on the Third Eye.

siddhasana sid-osunu (Sanskrit) "perfect posture" From a seated position, one heel is brought to the **perineum**, then the opposite ankle placed over the first with the toes and heel of the second foot resting in the fold between the thigh and calf of the first leg beneath it. The spine is held erect.

sushumna sush*umnu or **shushumna** shush*umnu (Sanskrit) "ascent" The central spinal channel.

sutra sūtru (Sanskrit) "suture or stitch" A short verse containing potent spiritual knowledge. When a group of such short verses are brought together, they "stitch" together the whole of knowledge.

Tantra tuntru (Sanskrit) "two woven together" Several books of esoteric doctrine, composed in the form of dialogs between Shiva and his Shakti.

Tao Dou (Chinese) "the way" The unitary first principle.

tapas tupus (Sanskrit) "heat, intensity"

Theosophical Society A society founded by Madame Blavatsky and others, in New York City in 1875, advocating a worldwide body of doctrine based largely on Brahmanic and Buddhistic teachings.

Theosophy The system of belief and practice of the Theosophical Society.

uddiyana ūdē*yonu (Sanskrit) "to fly up" A **yoga** practice involving the lifting of the abdomen with the diaphragm while the lungs are empty. This practice stimulates the higher functioning of the digestive system and raises **kundalini**.

Upanishads Ūp*anishadz (Sanskrit) "sitting down near" [secret doctrines] 108 commentaries on the **Vedas**, written in dialog form.

Vedas Vāduz (Sanskrit) "knowledge" The most ancient scriptures of India. There are four Vedas.

yoga yōgu (Sanskrit) "union" Not just a physical discipline, but also a mental discipline for attaining liberation from the material world and union of the self with the Supreme Being or ultimate principle.

yoni yōnē (Sanskrit) "female genitalia; womb"

Bibliography

Hall, Manly P. *The Secret Teachings of All Ages.* Self-published, 1928.

Hone, Mo. *The Seven Rays Today: A New Appreciation of the Ageless Wisdom and Esoteric Astrology.* Pluto Network, 2006.

   http://www.sevenraystoday.com

Hughes, Fred. *Am I Dead? ... or do I just feel like it*, Hobbies For Life, LLC, 2007.

Krishna, Gopi. *Kundalini: Evolutionary Energy in Man.* Berkeley: Shambala, p. 186, 1971.

Sannella, Lee, M.D. *The Kundalini Experience: Psychosis or Transcendence?.* Lower Lake, California: Integral Publishing, 1992.

Suggested Reading

Krishna, Gopi. *Kundalini: Evolutionary Energy in Man.* Berkeley: Shambala, 1971.

Newton, Michael. *Journey of Souls: Case Studies of Life Between Lives.* Llewellyn Publications, Woodbury, Minnesota, 1994.

——————. *Destiny of Souls: New Case Studies of Life Between Lives.* Llewellyn Publications, Woodbury, Minnesota, 2009.

Patanjali, *Yoga Sutras*

Vyasa, *Bhagavad Gita*

Yogananda, Paramhansa, *Autobiography of a Yogi.* The Philosophical Library, New York, 1946. Reprint: Crystal Clarity Publishers, Nevada City, California, 2005.